Bootstrap
CAPITAL

Bootstrap
CAPITAL

Microenterprises
and *the* American Poor

LISA J. SERVON

BROOKINGS INSTITUTION PRESS
Washington, D.C.

Library of Congress Cataloging-in-Publication data

Servon, Lisa J.
   Bootstrap capital : microenterprises and the American poor /
Lisa J. Servon.
      p.   cm.
   Includes bibliographical references and index.
   ISBN 0-8157-7806-6 (alk. paper)
   ISBN 0-8157-7805-8 (pbk. : alk. paper)
   1. Small business—United States. 2. Small business—United
States Case studies. 3. Small business—Government policy—United
States. 4. Small business—Government policy—United States Case
studies. I. Title.
   HD2346.U5 S47   1999   99-6513
   338.6'42'0973—dc21   CIP

9 8 7 6 5 4 3 2 1

Typeset in Sabon

Composition by Cynthia Stock
Silver Spring, Maryland

Printed by R. R. Donnelley and Sons
Harrisonburg, Virginia

research grant I received from the U.S. Department of Housing and Urban Development also helped me make my work truly relevant to public policy. Support from the Research Institute on Small and Emerging Businesses funded the chapter on self-employment as a strategy for welfare recipients, and the Mike Hogg research grant I received while at the University of Texas at Austin supported the work on social capital and the community development potential of the microenterprise strategy.

Sandra Acosta was an excellent assistant during the Accion New York phase of my research, particularly since most of her work consisted of interviewing people across the five boroughs in the summer heat while six months pregnant. In addition to doing solid work, Sandra gave me critical insight into the population and communities I studied in New York. Her own work on the Accion New York program added another dimension to mine. Thea Kayne worked with me during my year in Austin, and Jeffrey Doshna provided important assistance on this project at Rutgers University in New Jersey.

Innumerable advisers, friends, and colleagues read and commented on this work. Manuel Castells, my mentor and scholarly conscience, shaped the work from the beginning. Michael Teitz, AnnaLee Saxenian, and Troy Duster also provided invaluable insight and direction. Working with Norman Glickman, Susan Fainstein, Nancy Nye, Stephen Finn, and Bennett Harrison on community development research at the Center for Urban Policy Research at Rutgers University deepened my understanding of community development and enriched my understanding of microenterprise programs as community development programs. Ann Markusen's reading group at the Project on Regional and Industrial Economics at Rutgers University read and commented on chapter 6, and their perspective helped me sharpen that chapter. Tim Bates has contributed greatly to my macro understanding of the situation of entrepreneurs; working with him operated as an important check on my more fine-grained approach to this topic.

My understanding of the complexity of poverty and of poor peoples' lives was vastly expanded by the writings of Kathryn Edin, Michael Katz, Douglas Massey and Nancy Denton, Melvin Oliver, Michael Sherraden, Carol Stack, and William Julius Wilson. Their work, and the work of countless others, shaped the questions I asked and my approach to answering them. In addition, the students in my Urban Poverty and Community Development seminars, at Rutgers and at the University of Texas, continue to challenge and shape my understanding of these fields.

I thank my support network of family and friends for their encourage-

Acknowledgments

The world is made up of stories, not of atoms.

MURIEL RUKEYSER

I BEGIN BY THANKING the people working in the programs I studied for allowing me to poke around, ask questions, and get in the way. I hope my presence was not too obtrusive. In particular, I thank Etienne LeGrand and Barbara Johnson at the Women's Initiative for Self Employment (Women's Initiative); Jeff Ashe, Kim Wilson, and Karen Byron at Working Capital; Delma Soto and Hector Carino at Accion New York; Nancy Biberman and Donna Rubens at Women's Housing and Economic Development Corporation (WHEDCO); and Jason Friedman and John Else at the Institute for Social and Economic Development (ISED). These people are committed to the work they do and are intellectually curious about the impact their work has on those they serve. They let me into their offices, their files, and their homes. They opened many doors for me, providing me with access to their clients and others in the field who would have been nearly impossible to reach otherwise, and they spent hours talking with me about their triumphs, frustrations, and challenges.

Support from several sources enabled me to conduct this research. Generous funding from the Aspen Institute Nonprofit Sector Research Fund (NSRF), which also supported my attendance at the 1994 Association for Research on Nonprofit Organizations and Voluntary Associations (ARNOVA) conference, helped me place my work within the context of third sector research. Winning the Founder Region Fellowship from the Soroptimist International organization was as inspirational as it was helpful financially. The Soroptimists are a terrific bunch of women, and I thank them for believing in the worth of my work. The doctoral dissertation ment and their willingness to listen to me. Alec Gershberg has read this book more times than anyone and supported its evolution and my own completely. My parents, who are my biggest cheerleaders, have provided unconditional affirmation from the word "go." My sisters, Leslie and Jody, keep me grounded and always remind me where I came from. Many others along the way helped in myriad ways, offering necessary motivation, criticism, and insight. I can only list them here and apologize for those I have inadvertently overlooked: Bob Beauregard, Edward Blakely, Kaye Bock, Elke Davidson, Kathy Edin, Ted Egan, Gillian Hart, Marie Howland, Sarah Mabey, Rolf Pendall, Osman Shahenshah, Cas Stachelberg.

Most important, this research could not have been done without the participation of the entrepreneurs I interviewed. They let me into their homes and businesses and took valuable time away from their unbelievably busy schedules to tell me about their experiences and to share with me their triumphs, frustrations, battles, and dreams. This book is for and about them and the cities and communities across the country that they represent. My humble hope is that my current and future work can make some contribution toward giving them the opportunity to live fuller lives.

For Alec,
who opened the door,

and Manuel,
who showed the way

Contents

Abbreviations

AFDC	Aid for Families with Dependent Children
CARE	Cooperative for American Relief to Everywhere
CBOs	community-based organizations
CDBG	Community Development Block Grant
CDFI	Community Development Financial Institutions Fund
CfED	Corporation for Enterprise Development
CRA	Community Reinvestment Act
EOLs	economic opportunity loans
EZEC	Empowerment Zone/Enterprise Community
HUD	U.S. Department of Housing and Urban Development
HWEDP	Homeless Women's Economic Development Project
ICCD	Institute for Cooperative Community Development
ISED	Institute for Social and Economic Development
IWPR	Institute for Women's Policy Research
JOLI	Job Opportunities for Low-Income Individuals
JTPA	Job Training Partnership Act
LDCs	less developed countries
LMBC	Lawrence Minority Business Council
LRC	loan review committee
MOCD	Mayor's Office on Community Development
NCEP	National Community Economic Partnership
NGOs	nongovernmental organizations
OWBO	Office of Women's Business Ownership
PACE	People Acting in Community Endeavors

SBA	Small Business Administration
SEED	Self-Employment and Entrepreneurship Development
SEID	Self-Employment Investment Demonstration
SELP	Self-Employment Learning Project
TANF	Temporary Assistance for Needy Families
WEDI	Women's Economic Development Initiative
WEP	Work Experience Program
WEDCO	Women's Economic Development Corporation
WHEDCO	Women's Housing and Economic Development Corporation
WI	Women's Initiative for Self Employment
WSEP	Women's Self-Employment Project

ONE   *Introduction: Opportunity and Constraint*

DURING THE 1992 election campaign Bill Clinton called on Americans to "end welfare as we know it." This catch phrase elicited a strong response, for it succinctly captured a widely held belief: that the old welfare state no longer worked and that tinkering at the margins of poverty policy would no longer suffice. Indeed, such adjustments had not worked for a long time. Social security and other policies and programs created in the 1930s would soon be financially untenable over the long term. The War on Poverty and Great Society programs initiated in the early 1960s were crumbling under the weight of political criticism. But the lengthy sessions of Clinton's working group on welfare reform generated little action until August 1996 when, in anticipation of the upcoming election, the president signed legislation that replaced Aid for Families with Dependent Children (AFDC) with Temporary Assistance for Needy Families (TANF).[1]

There have been and continue to be reductions in major entitlement programs for the poor, such as AFDC, food stamps, supplemental security income for the elderly and disabled poor, and most forms of aid to legal immigrants. The structure of welfare is also changing sharply, now that benefits have a five-year lifetime limit and that at least 35 percent of recipients without young children must be working by 1999, a requirement that increases to 50 percent by 2002. Although these facts are no secret to

1. Also known as the Personal Responsibility and Work Opportunity Reconciliation Act of 1996 (P.L. 104-193).

anyone who has followed the development of welfare legislation, the larger meaning and probable long-term effects merit more thought than they have received.

According to the rhetoric of the New Right, the old welfare state caused aid recipients to depend on government assistance and gave them no incentive to become self-sufficient. In reality, the problem is not that the incentive has not existed, but that current policies and programs have consistently failed to illuminate the way out of dependency. Unfortunately, the new welfare legislation involves cutting current maintenance programs without figuring out how to replace them with strategies that teach people how to participate more fully in the mainstream economy. Perhaps most important, neither the old welfare state nor the recent reforms do what is most needed and what many other developed countries do: spend enough money on income redistribution. To move from reliance on welfare to economic self-sufficiency is a complex and lengthy process about which policymakers have much to learn. Microenterprise development—a relatively new strategy—provides a clear picture of what this process looks like for some of the persistent poor. It requires investing in people rather than simply maintenance. Since the 1930s, antipoverty policy has focused almost exclusively on maintenance.

And although before welfare reform there was a widespread consensus that the antipoverty policies of the 1930s and 1960s required serious reconstruction, the neoconservative pattern of using criticisms to justify the virtual removal of a public safety net is unacceptable. Welfare reform, coupled with recent changes in the way the economy works, underscores the need to train people to adapt to these changes rather than to develop skills that may not be useful in five years.

One of the most important of these changes is the phasing out of the unskilled from the U.S. work force, a trend that is also linked to a shift in the location of jobs. Responses to these changes have ranged from support for computer training programs to calls to relocate lower-skilled people from older industrial regions to areas where the demand for low-skilled workers is greater. Missing is the recognition that the fundamental structure of the economy has changed: that it has become more flexible, and that people must first establish a connection to the new structure and way of working before they can move forward in it. While building skills is certainly important, the kind of skills that programs must now teach include how to manage the constraints of the new economy, which means gaining access to information technology, economic literacy, and more flexible working conditions. Achieving this goal also requires something broader than teaching specifics. It is more about empowerment, which means allowing individuals to create the conditions by which to escape poverty. People cannot make this escape without help (as the neoconservatives maintain), nor can government do it for them (as the structure of the welfare state has historically implied).

This book examines one new strategy designed to help alleviate poverty and promote other economic development goals: microenterprise programs. Access to credit and training are two of the ingredients most lacking in U.S. areas with persistently high poverty levels. Microenterprise programs, which provide these two components, have quickly multiplied in response to this need. They see credit as a resource to which poor people have had difficulty gaining access. The Aspen Institute's *1996 Directory of U.S. Microenterprise Programs* profiles 328 programs in forty-six states that have assisted in the creation and growth of more than 36,000 businesses in 1995 alone, in large part among low-income people.[2] Microenterprise programs operate in both rural and urban settings; they target diverse populations, and their lending criteria differ from those used by mainstream financial institutions. Their single common denominator is that they serve as lenders of last resort, providing credit to people who want to be self-employed but who cannot obtain credit through traditional channels.[3] Microlenders make it their mission to take risks that fall outside those accepted by traditional banks. These programs seek to combat the idea that the poor are poor because they are lazy or otherwise deserving of their economic status.

The microenterprise strategy moved to the forefront of the U.S. policy agenda in early 1997, thanks to the international microcredit summit in Washington and to First Lady Hillary Rodham Clinton's decision to champion this issue as the Clinton administration began its second term. Policymakers and the media tout the microenterprise strategy as a way to alleviate poverty and create jobs in both the United States and in developing countries. Two thousand people from 110 countries attended the summit, which received unprecedented media coverage worldwide. Out of the summit came a U.S. commitment to support the microenterprise strategy with greater resources at home and abroad. The United States said it would

2. The actual number is likely higher, because the Aspen publication relies on survey respondents rather than a complete inventory of programs.

3. McLenighan and Pogge (1991).

triple current domestic spending on such programs and allocate as much as $1 billion over the next five years to U.S. community development projects that include microenterprise loans. In addition, a bipartisan group of twenty members of Congress introduced the Microcredit for Self-Reliance Act of 1997, in which $350 million would be allocated to the U.S. Agency for International Development to support microenterprise programs in developing countries.

Is the microenterprise strategy the silver bullet that will solve the world's poverty problems? Public officials at all levels in the United States are clamoring for ways to move poor people from public dependency to self-sufficiency, and the microenterprise strategy, with its bootstrap logic and impressive record in the developing world, has emerged as a promising front-runner in the race for new ideas. Neither the poverty problem nor the microenterprise solution is that simple, however.

Little study has been applied to how these programs work, where they fit within the context and history of programs designed to promote economic development and alleviate persistent poverty in the United States, and whom they serve. Although most media attention has cast the microenterprise strategy in a favorable light, wider debates surrounding the strategy have become polarized. On one hand, many are impressed with its bipartisan support, the high payback rates of existing lending programs, and the claim that, in theory at least, it can pay for itself. Proponents also claim that the programs provide disenfranchised populations with an entry point into the mainstream economy; the creation of new businesses and jobs that may subsequently result may also help revitalize low-income communities. On the other hand, some argue that the programs are expensive, that they fail to create many jobs, and that the jobs they do create are not good ones. These divergent positions tend to obscure the complex nature of the programs, the life situations of the populations they serve, and the relationships formed between lenders and borrowers. Both positions contain some element of truth. These complexities require closer examination to determine how the programs actually work, where they fit within traditional policy fields, and what contribution they can make to restructuring policy designed to alleviate persistent poverty.

This book fills this need by investigating five microenterprise programs currently in operation in the United States: Women's Initiative for Self Employment (Women's Initiative), which targets low- and moderate-income women in San Francisco and Oakland; Accion New York, which serves Latinos in New York City; Working Capital Metro Boston, which focuses on low-income entrepreneurs in the most troubled neighborhoods of Boston; the Institute for Social and Economic Development (ISED), which operates statewide in Iowa; and the Women's Housing and Economic Development Corporation (WHEDCO), which serves women in the New York City neighborhood of the South Bronx.

Women's Initiative for Self Employment

Women's Initiative for Self Employment (Women's Initiative) was initiated in September 1988 as a sponsored project of the Women's Foundation in San Francisco and was intended to increase the economic options available to women in the San Francisco Bay Area. The program provides entrepreneurial training, business and support services, and individual loans to low-income women. Its mission emphasizes training as a necessary component with which to facilitate the development and expansion of client businesses. The program offers four types of loans, ranging from research loans of up to $500 to growth loans of up to $20,000. Participants (with the exception of those applying for research loans, who may apply while attending classes) must complete fourteen weeks of training to qualify for a loan.

Accion New York

Founded in 1961 to work in community development in Latin America, Accion International was one of the pioneers in microenterprise assistance. When it recognized that the problems entrepreneurs in developing countries faced were similar to those experienced in the United States, it launched Brooklyn-based Accion New York as its first U.S. credit program. Six programs currently operate throughout the country.[4] Begun in July 1991, Accion New York serves the low-income Latino community in New York City by providing market-rate loans and basic business training to the self-employed. Loans are made both to groups and to individuals. Accion is a large, credit-led program that focuses on making loans to people who need little training to borrow but do not have access to credit through traditional channels. Accion's U.S. programs receive no public support so it can encourage local ownership of the programs. In addition, the six

4. For a recent evaluation of the Accion programs, see Himes and Servon (1998).

organizations form a network designed to provide each program with the benefits of power and collective strength.

Working Capital

Working Capital launched its first operations in rural New Hampshire in September 1990. Since then, the program has spread to areas of Maine, Vermont, New Hampshire, Massachusetts, Florida, and Delaware. The program expanded into the Boston area in 1992, and its Metro Boston project is the work examined here. Jeffrey Ashe, founder of Working Capital, modeled the program on Latin America's FINCA. Working Capital is highly decentralized and delegates much of the work done by staff in other programs to borrowers. All training and lending takes place within a peer group. The program was designed to serve low-income persons and economically distressed communities, but it does not exclude anyone from participating.

Institute for Social and Economic Development

John Else, a professor of social work at the University of Iowa, began the Institute for Social and Economic Development in 1988 after working in Zimbabwe for more than two years. There he helped train field staff who were carrying out the microenterprise strategy in rural areas. Recognizing the potential of this type of program for the United States, Else created ISED with initial funding from Iowa's Department of Economic Development, which was participating, along with four other states, in the Self-Employment Investment Demonstration. Jason Friedman, ISED's vice president of economic development, claims that ISED's program has four distinctive features, which differentiate it to some extent from other microenterprise programs: its historic focus on the welfare population, credit for clients obtained through commercial banks and public funds rather than its own loan fund, intensive follow-up after clients graduate, and holistic approach to business development. ISED does not have a loan program, but it does help participants obtain financing from other sources.

Women's Housing and Economic Development Corporation

The Women's Housing and Economic Development Corporation was begun in 1991 to promote economic independence of low-income women.

In addition to operating a microenterprise program, WHEDCO conducts job training. The corporation began its microenterprise activity relatively recently, and it is one of the few programs that focuses on a narrow strategy. It trains women to start businesses in one of two areas: food service and preparation, including catering and wholesale; and home-based child care. The program emphasizes broad entrepreneurial training similar to that provided by Women's Initiative and ISED, and in addition covers topics specific to its two sectors. Clients in the home-based daycare program, for example, can attend workshops on child safety and discipline.

Like Women's Initiative, WHEDCO targets low-income women. And like ISED, it does not do direct lending. Thus far the only source of funds participants have gained access to is Trickle Up, a private foundation, whose typical grant is $1,000.

Choice of Programs

Although all five programs focus on helping people use self-employment to become self-sufficient, each pursues that goal in a different way. The importance of credit within each program's larger mission differs greatly from one program to another (table 1-1).

According to a 1994 report based on data from the Aspen Institute's Self-Employment Learning Project, "There are three dimensions which, taken together, explain the range of diversity among U.S. microenterprise programs. These are: mission and anticipated outcomes; target population; and methodology."[5] The five programs discussed here vary across these three dimensions.

With respect to mission and anticipated outcomes, Women's Initiative and WHEDCO are oriented toward the individual economic empowerment of women, whereas Working Capital and ISED emphasize community empowerment. ISED and Women's Initiative are the programs most focused on people with very low income. Although Working Capital and Accion direct their resources toward the creation of strategies that will help the low-income self-employed, these programs do not exclude others who believe they can benefit from program services. Women's Initiative and WHEDCO also target women, and Accion New York targets Latinos. All three programs help businesses at different stages. Women's Initiative, WHEDCO, and ISED serve people who are starting businesses as well as

5. Klein (1994, p. 3).

Table 1-1. *Characteristics of Programs Studied*

Characteristic	Women's Initiative	Accion New York	Working Capital	ISED	WHEDCO
City or state	San Francisco/ Oakland	New York	Boston	Iowa	Bronx, N.Y.
Type of lending	Individual	Group and individual	Group	None	None
Target population	Low- and moderate- income women	Latinos	Low-income	Low-income	Low-income women
Type of business served	Start-ups and existing	Existing (one year or more)	Start-ups and existing	Start-ups and existing	Food and home- based child care businesses
Type of technical assistance	Classes and indivi- dual consulting	Individual con- sulting	Training within groups	Classes and indivi- dual consulting	...
Average loan size	$3,734	$3,069 in indivi- dual and $2,789 in groups	$891	...	...
Loan size range	$500 to $20,000		$500 to $5,000	...	...
Number of loans in 1995	23	140 in individual and 344 in groups	757	...	...

Source: Severens and Kays (1997).

those who have existing businesses, illustrating their greater focus on people than on business per se. Working Capital targets those who are already self-employed but allows individual groups to decide whether to lend to start-ups. Accion New York serves only those entrepreneurs who have been operating their business for at least one year, a decision that reflects the program's emphasis on business and entails taking on less risk.

Each program has also structured its training and lending somewhat differently. Microenterprise studies distinguish between credit-led programs (those that define their principal product as credit and focus on making loans) and training-led programs (those that concentrate on training and tend to have intensive and frequent interactions with their clients).[6] One can imagine a spectrum with prototypical economic development programs at one end and prototypical social welfare programs at the other, and with individual microenterprise programs plotted at different points along the spectrum. For most programs, the balance they achieve between training and lending by and large determines the place they occupy along the spectrum.

Of the programs studied here, Women's Initiative, WHEDCO, and ISED are training-led. Training-led organizations "tend to focus on microenterprise development as a way to help individuals living below the poverty line and on public assistance to achieve economic self-sufficiency."[7] Among the three, only Women's Initiative offers loans directly. Women's Initiative requires potential borrowers to take fourteen weeks of classes before applying for a loan, a rule that achieves the program's goal of increasing economic literacy and reflects its decision to work with start-up businesses. Although neither ISED nor WHEDCO makes loans, both programs help connect clients with alternative sources of business funding. Both also require clients to complete courses.

Accion New York and Working Capital are credit-led organizations. These programs "define their principal product as credit, and usually provide a limited amount of networking opportunities and training."[8] Accion New York does no formal training, although business consultants learn about client businesses during the loan process and often advise them on an individual basis. When Working Capital borrower groups are formed, they proceed through training exercises with the help of an enterprise agent;

6. Burrus and Stearns (1997).
7. Burrus and Stearns (1997, p. 7).
8. Burrus and Stearns (1997, p. 7).

the decision as to whether or not they will complete the training manual provided by Working Capital is left up to individual groups, however.

Current research on microenterprise programs and the people who use them fails to look closely enough at what these programs do, how they do it, and whom they serve. The basic tenet of this book is that the microenterprise strategy warrants close scrutiny on two levels: that of the program and that of the individual entrepreneur. The programs provide sorely needed insight that can help policymakers reconstruct the way in which they create and carry out antipoverty policy. On the individual level, the stories and experiences of those who use the microenterprise strategy provide a unique lens onto the life situations of poor people who are doing what they can to escape poverty. These stories help policymakers move beyond seeing the poor as a unified group, a necessary first step toward creating solutions to the problem of persistent poverty. Microenterprise programs and the people they serve are worth examining and learning from for a number of reasons.

The microenterprise strategy responds well to recent changes in large economic forces. Changes in national and global economic relations have for most people called into question the traditional path of going to college, getting a job, and keeping it for twenty or thirty years. Economic restructuring toward flexible specialization and an economy of small businesses have left many people without stable jobs that pay a living wage and provide necessary benefits. Programs and policies directed at urban poverty need to take these changes into account. The old model of training programs refers to a labor market that no longer exists for many job seekers, particularly the urban poor with few skills.

In reaction, many people are exploring self-employment because they believe it to be their best available option.[9] A woman in Iowa opened a consignment shop, which enabled her to leave welfare after having been laid off from her job in a meat-packing plant. Another patches income together from her home-based business services with other money she earns doing farm work in the harvest season and painting houses. Viewed from this perspective, microenterprise programs are perhaps the only ones targeting the persistent poor that respond to the constraints and opportunities posed by today's economic realities. Unlike most strategies designed to help the persistent poor, microenterprise programs help many people do a better job of something they are already doing to survive: starting

9. Servon (1998b).

small businesses or packaging income together from a variety of sources. Instead of trying to channel poor people into a mainstream economy that is no longer a reality, they teach those with an interest in and inclination for self-employment how to strengthen their entrepreneurial skills and stabilize their businesses.

Microenterprise programs mobilize people and address the problem of economic restructuring and its effect on the labor market. The programs motivate people who are interested in taking responsibility for their own lives and futures and try to provide them with the tools they will need to make that happen. The personal relations skills the programs breed, particularly during the borrowing process, also help program participants take advantage of other programs and create critical support networks. In addition to helping people start and stabilize businesses rather than preparing them for dead-end or nonexistent jobs, microenterprise programs help prove to people that with access to the right resources they can do something useful that also engages them. Making this connection is the first step toward the goal of participating fully in society: economically, politically, and socially.

The microenterprise strategy can influence the reconstruction of other policies and programs designed to alleviate poverty. The microenterprise strategy breaks out of the box imposed by the boundaries of traditional policy fields. In particular, it brings to discussions of policy reform a marriage of agendas for economic development and poverty alleviation, for it derives from a philosophy that blurs the lines between these two goals. Economic development is generally concerned with job creation but usually on a much larger scale than microenterprise programs accomplish. Poverty alleviation typically has to do with moving people off welfare and into the work force and frequently focuses on "reforming" individual and family characteristics to accomplish that goal. Microenterprise programs tend to work with individuals as they are, rather than try to reform them.

More important, antipoverty policy has historically treated poverty as a problem largely apart from other policy arenas. This attitude goes back at least as far as the New Deal, when public assistance was perceived as a way to tide people over until the economy picked up. When the War on Poverty began thirty years later, economic conditions were much better, allowing a different kind of separation to take place. The economy was growing, and policymakers assumed that it would continue to grow. War on Poverty programs emphasized job training and education to improve employability and civil rights to open up opportunity. This focus on individual rehabilitation rather than redistribution distinguished the War on Poverty from the New Deal. However, antipoverty policy continued to remain separate from national economic policy, for although the New Deal dole was thought of as a temporary measure, the architects of the War on Poverty believed that the economy would continue to absorb new workers. The economic surplus also implied that it would be relatively easy to continue to fund the programs for as long as they were necessary. In fact, the persistence of poverty despite public assistance efforts and periods of national and urban economic recovery implies that a more complex dynamic is in place.

The War on Poverty set the precedent of combating poverty by reforming individuals' characteristics rather than setting the fundamentals of economic organization at the core of poverty alleviation policy. Social and cultural conditions as well as political and economic conditions require examination. Poverty is a multifaceted problem that intersects with many policy spheres. Hybridized programs that combine elements of these policy areas can provide direction for drafting other programs designed to alleviate persistent poverty. As an example, ISED, one of the most savvy microenterprise programs, has formed critical relationships with the state departments of economic development and human services.

Microenterprise programs create networks that build social capital in areas that need it most. The programs build two types of networks: within and between programs. Those within programs consist of the relationships formed among borrowers and between borrowers and program staff. Interprogram networks consist of the links forged with other community-based organizations as well as institutions in the public and private sectors.

These networks are mutually reinforcing. As both WISE and Working Capital demonstrate, this interaction forms a virtuous cycle in which the empowerment of individuals within programs enables borrowers to demand access to other organizations and institutions, which may include banks, community colleges, and social welfare agencies. The learning that occurs through the interaction between these other institutions and microenterprise programs makes them more accessible to borrowers.

The relationships formed between microenterprise programs and other organizations link program participants to critical service providers. Accion helps borrowers with immigration issues; Women's Initiative has strong relationships with other social service agencies. Potential microentrepreneurs, especially those who are among the persistent poor, often require services that extend beyond access to credit and training. These relationships also increase the visibility and reach of programs.

Microenterprise programs help a segment of the welfare population leave poverty through self-employment. Self-employment alone is unlikely to provide low-income people with the economic security they need. Most microentrepreneurs engage in self-employment in combination with other wage and salary jobs or a second self-employment job, and their self-employment activity provides smaller annual earnings than does their wage or salary work.[10] Why, then, pursue self-employment at all? Because the people microenterprise programs target often have trouble obtaining enough wage or salary work to meet their needs. Full-time jobs with benefits that pay enough to support families are becoming more scarce; for those with the fewest opportunities, self-employment often makes the difference between poverty and self-sufficiency. A woman has been laid off from her union job printing newspapers and has decided to open a used furniture shop while picking up shifts at her old plant when she can. She cannot find full-time work that will provide comparable pay and benefits. Many microentrepreneurs, particularly women, use self-employment as part of an income-packaging strategy in which they combine paid employment, receipt of means-tested welfare benefits, and income from additional sources. A California couple supplements the money they make from their chutney and spice company with catering, yard work, and child care. Some microentrepreneurs choose self-employment over work for wages because they prefer to work for themselves or because it allows them to work at home and combine other responsibilities, such as child care, with income generation. When his wife left, an Iowa man quit his job because he could not travel as much as the job required and still take care of his two children. He opened a television repair shop and moonlights at a bar when he needs to supplement his business income. Many microentrepreneurs expand and contract their self-employment activity according to the availability of other work.

Organization of the Book

The book follows a sort of chronological flow of process and outcome. It begins by discussing how and why the microenterprise strategy came into existence in the United States. The purpose here is to show how contem-

10. Spalter-Roth, Soto, and Zandniapour (1994, p. 4).

porary U.S. microenterprise programs differ in critical ways from earlier alternative lending programs and from the developing world examples to which they are generally compared. The next step is to review the research on the microenterprise strategy. The focus then shifts to outcomes, as reflected in case studies of the five microenterprise programs already described. Specific points of interest are the ways they blend aspects of more traditional economic development and social welfare, the potential for self-employment among those reliant on welfare, and the potential for community development through the direct and indirect effects of the microenterprise strategy.

The book concludes by reconsidering whether and how these programs should be supported. It also looks at the characteristics that make the programs successful and explores the idea of creating other hybrid programs blending economic development and social welfare with these characteristics as a base.

The voices of microenterprise clients, field experts, program staff, and policymakers quoted throughout this book testify to the variety of outcomes the microenterprise strategy generates and the complex way these programs pursue their missions. Conclusions about the strategy are made largely on the basis of the stories told by nearly eighty people who have pursued self-employment through microenterprise programs. These stories are not sufficient to judge the efficacy of a complicated strategy that is continuing to evolve. Instead, the book describes and explains this complexity in a way that will inform future policy designed to help the persistent poor.

TWO   *Learning from History*

MOST OF THE people attracted to the microenterprise strategy exist at the margins of the mainstream economy. They include the working poor, those who have found themselves jobless as a result of economic restructuring, those who cannot make ends meet from the part-time and temporary work that is increasingly replacing full-time work and its benefits, and those who find corporate America currently inaccessible or undesirable for any one of a number of reasons. The people who start businesses through these programs do so largely because they need more money. Most use the extra income their businesses generate to survive. Few get rich.

In an effort to meet the needs of these new entrepreneurs, microenterprise programs are being created at a fast pace, with public and private support. The microenterprise strategy derives from two main precepts: that self-employment is becoming an ever more important segment of the economy, particularly for groups whose ability fully to participate in the mainstream economy is somehow restricted; and that microentrepreneurs face market barriers that constrain the successful operation of their businesses. If self-employment is to be a real option for disadvantaged populations, policymakers need to know more about the people these programs are serving and how they work.

Precedents for Microenterprise Programs

Current U.S. programs have their roots both in less developed countries (LDCs) and in past U.S. programs. Popular perceptions and the results

15

reported from programs based in LDCs have created specific expectations for these programs that are often inappropriate.

Programs in the Developing World

The story of the microenterprise strategy begins in Bangladesh where in 1979 economics professor Mohammed Yunus initiated the Grameen Bank.[1] The bank is perhaps the closest thing to a household name in the microenterprise world.[2] Yunus developed his trademark methodology of group lending as a way to help the landless poor start businesses without having to rely on usurious moneylenders. The strategy of group lending, or peer lending as it is sometimes called, boosts network formation in disadvantaged communities. With group lending, four to ten people who currently operate or desire to operate their own businesses form a group, receive training together, and decide who will receive the first loan. The trust of fellow members serves as collateral. Other members receive loans and achieve eligibility for additional loans only as long as all members maintain current payments. Both in developing and developed countries, women make up the vast majority of peer lending groups. Group lending may constitute the most tangible example of how these programs, under particular circumstances, can foster networks similar to those that have made certain ethnicity-based lending and savings groups so successful. Providing support to groups rather than to individuals builds community and therefore serves both social and economic aims.

The Grameen Bank currently operates more than 1,050 branch offices that serve 35,000 villages and 2 million customers; loans are administered by more than 10,000 university and high school graduates.[3] After eighteen years of this alternative lending activity, the bank has disbursed more than $1 billion; the repayment rate is an impressive 97 percent.

The Grameen Bank also pioneered the concept of combining economic development with social welfare objectives. In addition to attending group meetings geared toward helping them learn how to run their businesses, borrowers attend lectures on sanitation, nutrition, and other topics relevant to their lives. They also agree to adhere to the Sixteen Principles,

---

1. The United States has funded these LDC programs throughout their history through USAID, UNDP, and other organizations. It has been much more difficult to obtain public funding for U.S. programs.
2. Bornstein (1996).
3. Bornstein (1996).

which include pledging to boil water and refusing to participate in the country's economically crippling dowry system. Many other programs in the United States and abroad offer social services geared toward the needs of their target populations. The Lakota Fund in South Dakota helps participants address alcoholism, for example, and Freedom from Hunger in Mali and Ghana provides education on hunger prevention.

Since 1983, when Yunus institutionalized his program with the aid of government authorities and commercial bankers, group lending has become popular throughout the developing world, and several programs have reached similar scales and repayment rates. The microenterprise strategy quickly spread from Bangladesh throughout less developed countries in Asia, Africa, and Latin America. The programs marked a change in strategy from large trickle-down efforts to smaller bottom-up techniques. The new emphasis had "the support of both conservative governments promoting free markets and more progressive nongovernmental organizations (NGOs) intrigued by the informal survival tactics of the poor."[4] Countries adapted to their individual circumstances the basic concept of providing small amounts of credit to poor entrepreneurs depending on their needs. As a result, programs worldwide exhibit remarkable variety, which is testimony to the flexibility of the strategy.

Contexts in the United States and the Developing World

The remarkable results and rapid growth achieved in LDC-based programs caught the attention of U.S. policymakers and organizers in the mid-1980s. Although the policymakers were unaccustomed to looking to the developing world for solutions to domestic social problems, the success of these programs, coupled with the increasing recognition of unmet credit and training needs among poor people in the United States, made this idea difficult to ignore. In addition, Americans such as Jeff Ashe, founder of Working Capital, who has spent more than twenty years establishing programs in developing countries, became convinced that the microenterprise strategy could work in the United States. Ashe and others began to knock on the doors of domestic funders and policymakers and became persuasive spokespeople for a U.S. microenterprise movement.

Conversations such as those that took place at the February 1997 Microcredit summit in Washington moved from the African rain forest to

4. Mt. Auburn Associates (1994, pp. 2–5).

the asphalt of the South Bronx. Although it is encouraging that U.S. policymakers have begun to look outside U.S. borders for ways to combat persistent poverty, differences in economic, political, and social contexts between the developed and developing worlds deeply affect the potential and limits of the microenterprise strategy for the United States.

Yet there are some noteworthy similarities between the contexts in the United States and abroad and the resulting programs. These include a population that is inadequately served by mainstream financial institutions, women who need economic alternatives, and intractable and persistent poverty. Whether in the United States or in Bangladesh, more people need credit than can obtain it. Individuals in both developed and less developed countries have the energy, drive, and wherewithal to start businesses. And in both contexts, the act of giving credit to a motivated, disenfranchised, potential entrepreneur can be a powerful step toward self-sufficiency.

At the same time, starting a microenterprise program in a developed country is much different—and in many ways more difficult—than making it work in a less developed country. Perhaps the most significant difference is the prevalence and strength of the informal economy in less developed countries. Although an informal sector certainly exists in the United States, it is neither as vital nor as accepted here as it is in the developing world. The public sector in many less developed countries supports microenterprise programs that assist informal businesses, whereas the U.S. government penalizes people for operating their businesses under the table.

Entrepreneurs in the United States also need economic literacy to deal with the complex regulatory environment surrounding business ownership. Working in the formal economy means filing tax returns; it also may mean completing licensing, certification, and inspection requirements. A child care or food-related business in the United States must undergo inspections and meet licensing requirements that are not as likely to be required in the developing world. Furthermore, U.S. entrepreneurs require more capital and more advanced training than their counterparts in the developing world. The Grameen Bank's average initial loan is $60; loans through Bolivia-based Banco Sol, another well-established program, average $212. Loans at Women's Initiative, Working Capital, and Accion New York average $3,255, $824, and $1,500, respectively, and neither ISED nor WHEDCO makes loans. Even at these levels, some researchers and borrowers believe that the loan sizes are too small and that the businesses remain forever disadvantaged by undercapitalization.[5]

---

5. Numbers come from sources at programs. See also Bates (1995).

Another notable difference is the sharper growth of LDC-based programs. One reason for this is that many of the borrowers in less developed countries are already entrepreneurs, whereas many of the U.S. businesses are start-ups. Another is that U.S. programs must allocate much more of their budgets toward training, which is expensive, whereas LDCs can focus on lending. With their necessary emphasis on training, U.S. programs will continue to require heavy subsidization from government and private for-profit and nonprofit organizations. This difference in the balance between training and lending results in part from the need to work in the formal economy, which requires greater economic literacy than the informal economy. In addition, self-employment is less prevalent in the United States than in the developing world. Low-income entrepreneurs here are likely to have grown up knowing more public assistance recipients than entrepreneurs. In the developing world, where there is no public assistance, self-employment is the only safety net or survival strategy many people have. As pointed out in a 1992 report for the Rockefeller Foundation, "The *tradition* of welfare as opposed to that of microenterprise can not be overestimated as a major obstacle to encouraging enterprise development and borrowing among the poor."[6] Now that the safety net in the United States has begun to disintegrate because of welfare reform, policymakers at all levels of government have come to consider self-employment as a way to move welfare recipients off public assistance.

Finally, the microenterprise movement in LDCs is characterized by support from large national and international programs (many of which receive substantial resources from U.S. and internationally based aid organizations), while the microenterprise movement in the United States consists mainly of small, local programs. A few U.S. programs have begun to grow aggressively; two of the most notable are Accion and Working Capital, both of which operate in several states. Interestingly, both have strong ties to foreign programs. Accion was created and deployed in Latin America in 1973, before it was transferred to Brooklyn in 1991. Jeff Ashe, founder and director of Working Capital, worked in the microenterprise movement throughout the developing world before initiating his U.S. program, which, as already mentioned, is modeled after Latin America's FINCA. And Ashe continues to consult with developing countries on matters of alternative credit, maintaining a continuing connection between the activities at Working Capital and in LDCs.

As a result of all these factors, U.S. programs are far more expensive to

6. Novogratz (1992, p. 14).

maintain and slower to expand than their LDC counterparts. This does not necessarily mean that support for U.S. programs should be decreased. Rather, the contextual differences must create differences in expectations. The news media in particular are guilty of portraying the microenterprise story as a seamless development from Bangladesh to Bedford Stuyvesant.[7]

Although LDC-based programs have achieved incredible size in a short time, the same growth is unlikely to occur in the United States. The largest U.S. programs do not even approach the scale of the Grameen Bank and Banco Sol programs. According to Katherine McKee, head of the microenterprise division of the U.S. Agency for International Development (USAID), those who run alternative financial institutions must seriously address the problem of sustainability. McKee acknowledges the difficult balancing act of "trying to run a microloan fund so as to achieve break-even, while doing business the regular financing market finds unprofitable." As she asserts, "Institution managers will have to take a hard-nosed approach and make very difficult trade-offs if they want their institutions to survive and grow—and continue to achieve the goals for which they were created."[8] For the most part these trade-offs involve cost-cutting and serving borrowers less broadly and deeply. To increase their odds for survival, McKee recommends that they use peer borrowing, keep overhead costs low, streamline the paperwork as much as possible, standardize their loan products, simplify loan administration and servicing, refuse to subsidize the loans, diversify risks, seek as much grant funding for capital and reserves as possible, and get the most out of lending activity.

Other researchers and field experts believe that size is not the most important issue.[9] Rather than aspiring to match the very large LDC programs, U.S. programs need an alternative model with different indicators of success. Some question whether sustainability is even possible. According to Chris Sikes of the Western Massachusetts Enterprise Fund, "It will never be that way. If you are casting microenterprise development as a poverty-alleviation strategy, it will never be self-sustaining." The Aspen Institute, which has conducted some of the only longitudinal research on microenterprise programs, recently mounted its Microtest initiative, which works with microenterprise practitioners to determine appropriate measurement and evaluation standards. Some observers believe that micro-

7. Bornstein (1995); Cooper (1992).
8. McKee (1990, p. 14).
9. Clark and Kays (1995, pp. 3–4).

enterprise programs do need to ensure their own sustainability, but that in the United States it will not be the result of large size. Instead, program directors have begun to diversify loan portfolios and take on new activities that will generate funds to support their microenterprise development work.

U.S. Policy Efforts

Although the microenterprise strategy is presented here as something new, lending and business training programs do appear sporadically throughout the history of public policy directed at both local economic development and poverty alleviation. During the late 1960s the Model Cities program attempted to generate businesses that would employ poor people, although there was no requirement that they be run by the poor. About the same time, the Small Business Administration (SBA) extended many thousands of economic opportunity loans (EOLs) to poor people, "few [of whom] possessed the necessary skills, education, or work experience that successful business operation commonly requires."[10] This program is the closest U.S. precedent for current microenterprise programs, although there are critical differences. The EOL program, which routinely lent as much as $25,000, failed to provide much training or to address the needs that these entrepreneurs had in addition to credit. As a result, rates of loan delinquency and default were very high. The structure of current programs shows that the lessons from these earlier programs have been learned. Nearly all U.S. microenterprise programs include a training component, which in many cases dominates the lending activity. And although microlenders do make loans that traditional financial institutions consider too risky, the process is slow and careful. Lenders make efforts to know potential borrowers and their commitment to their businesses. In addition, initial loan amounts are very small: a maximum of $5,000 from Women's Initiative (but as low as $200) and a mere $500 from Working Capital.

The business assistance programs that followed equal opportunity loans in the 1970s and 1980s were funded either through the Community Development Block Grant (CDBG) program in the Department of Housing and Urban (HUD) Development, or through the Department of Labor, as mandated by the Job Training Partnership Act (JTPA). Other programs through the Economic Development Administration focused more on attracting business rather than generating it.

10. Bates (1995).

In the middle to late 1980s, the U.S. microenterprise strategy began to evolve as a result of grass roots efforts. According to Robert Friedman, executive director of the Corporation for Enterprise Development, its initial concern was to help women who found themselves having to manage both the social and economic needs of their households. Indeed, the first program, Women's Economic Development Corporation (WEDCO), was for women. And, although the media generally locate the roots of the U.S. microenterprise movement in the Grameen Bank and other programs in developing countries, some observers believe that the more direct link is to WEDCO (now called Women Venture). The Minneapolis-based program was founded in 1983 by Kathy Keeley, a woman who has been called the mother of the U.S. microenterprise movement. From the outset, it explicitly combined economic development and social welfare goals. According to Bob Friedman, executive director of the Corporation for Enterprise Development (CfED), "Kathy had them write child care into the business plan. . . . The more holistic, more flexible view always combines business and financial skills on the one hand, and is also concerned with family and personal development." The Women's Self-Employment Project (WSEP), the second oldest program in the country, considered itself a hybrid of Women Venture and the Grameen Bank.

In recent years the public sector has shown increasing interest in employing microenterprise programs to generate economic activity and alleviate poverty. One of the first poverty alleviation programs was the Job Opportunities for Low-Income Individuals (JOLI) program, administered by the Office of Community Services in the Department of Health and Human Services. Started in 1990, JOLI provides three-year grants to non-profit organizations engaging in demonstration projects aimed at creating jobs for low-income people, particularly welfare recipients. In fiscal 1997 the program received an appropriation of $5.5 million, which enables it to make ten three-year grants of up to $500,000. To date eighty-one programs across the country have been funded.

Another program, the Micro-Enterprise Development Project in the Office of Refugee Resettlement of the Department of Health and Human Services, awards grants to states and public or private nonprofit organizations providing microenterprise services to refugees. Targeted refugees include those receiving public assistance, at risk for receiving public assistance, and lacking the ability to secure small loans. The Office of Refugee Resettlement provided more than $2.3 million in grants in fiscal 1996.

The Small Business Credit and Business Opportunity Enhancement Act of 1992 includes a $15 million microenterprise demonstration program.

In addition, HUD recently allocated funds to help participants in their programs become self-employed, primarily through CDBG funding. A significant increase in federal funding occurred in 1992, coincident with the beginning of the Clinton administration, and the CDBG program created a category specifically for microenterprise programs. Although CDBG funds come from the federal government, the grants are administered by city or state governments.

More recently, the Empowerment Zone and Enterprise Communities programs, also administered by HUD's Office of Community Planning and Development, have provided some support for microenterprise development. These programs provide incentives to enable communities to improve economic opportunities in distressed urban neighborhoods and rural areas. Many communities have included microenterprise training and lending activities in their plans.

The SBA's Microloan Demonstration Program, begun in 1992, made twenty-five loans available that year to microenterprise programs and forty in 1993. Microenterprise programs that wanted to serve greater numbers of clients and extend their range of services, as well as other community economic development programs with little lending experience, eagerly applied for the loans. When asked how much the SBA had increased its microenterprise loan pool from its first year to its second, Jody Raskind, an SBA official, replied, "Let's put it this way: Two years ago there was nothing. Now we have $85 million to lend out."

Several elements of this SBA initiative met with some skepticism among more experienced programs, however. First, the SBA packaged this funding primarily as loans, not grants, meaning that programs would eventually be required to repay. Second, most of the money had to be earmarked for programs' loan funds; it could not be used to fund training and other operating expenses. And if the funded program failed to make enough loans, it lost the money. Most programs that focus on training, as the earlier EOL program shows they should do, already have more money in their loan funds than they can use; what they really need is more help with operating expenses. Third, the SBA required that programs make loans of up to $25,000—a much greater sum than many programs are accustomed to lending—and put pressure on them to make loans in the upper limits of the range, which may have spurred programs to make bad loans. But according to Julia Vindasius, former director of the Arkansas-based Good Faith Fund, the stipulations attached to this program are not without their advantages. The "use it or lose it" requirement caused Vindasius and her staff to be more creative about devising new types of loans. At the same time, these requirements potentially encourage programs to change their target populations, make bad loans, and lend clients more than they may be capable of repaying. Recently, the SBA added technical assistance funding to its range of supports, making grants of approximately $125,000 to microenterprise programs that do not make loans.

Another source of microenterprise support within the SBA has been the Office of Women's Business Ownership (OWBO). The OWBO administers centers to provide women with information, expertise, and training and technical assistance. It has sixty-three centers in thirty-six states, Puerto Rico, and the District of Columbia. The client base is economically diverse, ranging from welfare recipients to women with moderate incomes, and also ethnically diverse, with 40 percent consisting of minorities. Some microenterprise organizations that specifically serve women have received funds from the OWBO.

In 1992 the federal government made existing relationships between the microenterprise movement and the JTPA and CDBG programs more explicit. Legislation was enacted that designates self-employment training as an allowable JTPA activity and authorizes a microenterprise demonstration within the JTPA system. Additional legislation strongly encourages CDBG recipients to devote 1 percent of their funds to capitalizing microenterprises.[11]

In 1994 three new federal initiatives in alternative lending were created. The National Community Economic Partnership (NCEP), a program of the Department of Health and Human Services, targets the urban and rural poor, providing credit to community development corporations for revolving loan funds that support microentrepreneurs. The Riegle Act, which focuses on small-scale entrepreneurs, provides financing to states that encourage banks to lend to small businesses.

A third major piece of legislation was the Community Development Banks and Financial Institutions Act. Its stated purpose was to create "a network of community development banks whose primary mission is to lend, invest, and provide basic banking services in low- and moderate-income communities."[12] The president's 1996 budget proposed $144 million for these community-based institutions with the intention that the funds would be used to generate matching grants from local community development agencies and the private financial sector. Although this act is

11. Charles Stewart Mott Foundation (1993, p. 13).
12. HUD (1994 p. 36).

not targeted specifically to microentrepreneurs, the president's 1995 urban policy report does cite entrepreneurs as one of the groups it is intended to benefit. The larger goal is that "these local financial intermediaries will connect communities to mainstream financial sources and unleash the private sector to help rebuild communities that want to help themselves."[13]

This legislation created the Community Development Financial Institutions Fund (CDFI), which operates as part of the Department of the Treasury. The CDFI program makes grants, loans, and other investments in community development financial institutions, which include community development banks, credit unions, loan funds, venture capital funds, and microenterprise loan funds. In the first round, in July 1996, the CDFI awarded $37.2 million to thirty-two institutions, among them two microenterprise organizations and several other institutions that include microlending as part of their community financing effort.

The administration is encouraging the CDFI to take the lead in microenterprise development. A 1995 executive order charged it with implementing two programs especially directed toward microenterprises. The first is the Presidential Awards for Excellence in Microenterprise Development and the second an interagency effort to coordinate microenterprise programs administered by the federal agencies and departments. The CDFI recently convened the first formal meeting of the interagency effort. In June 1998, with full support from the administration, Senators Edward Kennedy, Pete Domenici, Bob Kerrey, and Jeff Bingaman introduced S2190 to authorize "qualified organizations to provide technical assistance and capacity building services to microenterprise development organizations and programs and to disadvantaged entrepreneurs using funds from the Community Development Financial Institutions Fund."

At the same time that CDFI was being established, the Community Reinvestment Act (CRA), which was passed in 1977 but failed to accomplish its mission, was subsequently rewritten to include new implementing regulations to give it teeth. The Financial Institutions Reform, Recovery, and Enforcement Act, which mandated changes in the CRA, was passed in 1989. The goal of the CRA is and always has been to encourage lending institutions to serve the needs of creditworthy borrowers in their communities. Its new provisions have made it more responsive to the credit needs of a broader clientele; this activity has continued during the Clinton administration. If effective, the improved CRA should make traditional fi-

13. HUD (1994, p. 37).

nancial institutions more receptive to serving the needs of those who had been served only through alternative lending institutions such as microenterprise programs. And in February 1997 the United States hosted the international "microcredit summit" at which both President and Mrs. Clinton strongly supported U.S. and international programs. A second summit was held in New York City in June 1998. The realization of the programs initiated during the Clinton administration is still in the works, which makes it too soon to evaluate their effectiveness, but the volume and scope of the recent efforts clearly mark a swell of support for microenterprise programs and microentrepreneurs.

Although this entry of government into the provision of microenterprise training and lending is significant for the microenterprise movement, none of the new public programs has staked a very large claim on the strategy in comparison with other efforts. All seem to be hedging their bets by funding small demonstration programs or limited efforts without promising to incorporate the strategy into long-term efforts. Still, microenterprise programs are receiving a greater percentage of their budgets from public sources than they were when they started: a survey of ten microenterprise programs showed that between 1987 and 1992, public funding rose from 15.9 to 40.6 percent of their budgets.[14]

What impact will this surge in public funding have on microenterprise programs? The increased support has garnered media attention across the board, from the *Wall Street Journal* to *Rolling Stone Magazine*. Thus far, however, there has been no recognition of the two-faced nature of greater public involvement. Indeed, the expansion of government participation represents an important step in the institutionalization of microenterprise, both on the purely beneficial side of giving the strategy greater stability and an aura of legitimacy and from the less clear perspective that it may help create a model not directly in keeping with the needs of programs. With the increasing use of federal funds comes federal control and federal standards, which may distort program missions. These may be standards of process, such as public participation, or standards of outcome, such as default rates and loan volume. Many program advocates are concerned that such standards will constrain local creativity by imposing greater homogeneity.[15]

14. Servon (1994).
15. Servon (1994).

In addition, elements of current policy still create barriers to self-employment, particularly for people receiving welfare who are interested in entrepreneurship. Before welfare reform, the barriers consisted of a $1,000 limit on the assets of AFDC recipients, which effectively prohibited them from accumulating the assets needed to run a business; a limit of $1,500 net equity value in a vehicle; a practice of counting business assets as personal resources, making it difficult for an entrepreneur to keep business and personal accounts separate; a rule prohibiting self-employed AFDC recipients from deducting costs of capital, purchases, depreciation, and repayments of loan capital in calculating gross countable income; and a loss of benefits if an AFDC recipient worked more than 100 hours a month.[16] Some states have begun to change the regulations. The introduction of welfare reform has generated an array of experiments related to self-employment. In New York and many other states, work requirements are interrupting low-income entrepreneurs' attempts to use self-employment to move off welfare. In most states, even those that have made regulations more favorable for recipients pursuing self-employment, recipients who start businesses lose their benefits before their business is large enough and stable enough to support them. Many of the federal programs that do support microenterprise programs, such as JTPA, "force microenterprise programs to fit themselves within a job-training rather than a business development framework."[17]

Barriers exist at the local level as well. Although the community seems the most appropriate entity to deliver microenterprise program services, because it allows for flexibility of program design, local human service agencies have been inconsistent in their cooperation when asked to work with microenterprise programs in serving public assistance recipients. According to some program representatives, "The majority of Private Industry Councils have found little incentive within the JTPA system, besides authorizing language, to use funds for microenterprise training. Restrictive zoning and erratic CRA compliance also have undermined attempts for programs to fund home-based businesses and secure participation from local banks."[18]

16. Corporation for Enterprise Development (1993, pp. 7–8).
17. Charles Stewart Mott Foundation (1994, p. 17).
18. Charles Stewart Mott Foundation (1993, p. 13).

Conclusion

Making comparisons between current U.S. microenterprise programs and past U.S. programs or LDC programs is not necessarily appropriate and must always be done carefully. Still, the programs continue to be grouped together in both the popular and academic press. Although it is important to study and draw lessons from their similarities and differences, the great danger is that the programs will be judged against inappropriate standards. The differences manifested in this new set of alternative lending programs and the people who use them therefore need to be approached with caution.

Microenterprise programs depart in important ways from previous attempts to address the problem of persistent poverty through economic development. They are more flexible, more creative, and more oriented to the context in which they operate than either traditional economic development or poverty alleviation strategies. Indeed, the microenterprise strategy offers hope that there is room to maneuver within the confines of policies now in place. Perhaps the current changeful political and economic environment offers an opportunity to accommodate a greater array of responses. Before leaping at this chance, however, it is important to understand the critical differences between U.S. and LDC programs and to build on what has been learned from EOLs and other earlier programs. Chapter 3 begins this in-depth examination with a closer look at the microenterprise strategy.

THREE *Programs,*
Businesses, and
Entrepreneurs

A BROAD OVERVIEW of current microenterprise activi-
ties in the United States and their outcomes can be gleaned from studies of
the subject thus far, though they are few in number and vary greatly in
their quality, scope, and emphasis (which ranges from the programs to the
entrepreneurs to the businesses). Nevertheless, they set the stage for the
finer-grained and more analytical work in the chapters that follow. This
chapter summarizes the findings from the most useful of these studies.
Because the studies are heavily cited, it seems appropriate at this point to
describe the scope and orientation, as well as the shortcomings, of each.

One of these research efforts is the Self-Employment Learning Project
(SELP), established at the Aspen Institute in 1991 with funding from the
Charles Stewart Mott and Ford Foundations. SELP began as a study of
five well-established programs. The Ms. Foundation joined SELP the following year, adding two programs from its Collaborative for Women's
Economic Development. The SELP effort studied these seven programs
over a five-year period ending in December 1996. It generated and ana-
lyzed several data sources, including interviews of 405 entrepreneurs served
by the programs, a program profile that aggregates data on all program
clients from each of the participating programs, and two sets of case studies of each agency that were completed in 1992 and 1994. Because only a
small number of programs was studied, caution must be exercised in drawing generalizations from SELP's results. SELP is undeniably important
because it is the only longitudinal study of the microenterprise strategy

and it provides a comprehensive look at programs, entrepreneurs, and businesses.[1]

The Self-Employment Investment Demonstration (SEID) evaluation began in 1986, cosponsored by the Corporation for Enterprise Development (CfED), along with five states (Iowa, Maryland, Michigan, Minnesota, and Mississippi), which allowed welfare recipients to continue to receive benefits for one year while they established businesses.[2] SEID focused on the entrepreneurs rather than the programs.[3] The purpose of the demonstration was to determine if self-employment could be a route to self-sufficiency for welfare recipients and to identify policy barriers to economic self-sufficiency for this population.[4] The primary evaluation of SEID consists of a postprogram follow-up study conducted in 1994 to identify outcomes for a random sample of SEID participants who started businesses.[5] Unfortunately, the evaluation does not look at what happened to those who did not start businesses.[6]

The *Small Steps toward Big Dreams* series is based on annual surveys of the programs funded by the Charles Stewart Mott Foundation.[7] The foundation published the first report in the series in 1990; updates were published annually from 1991 through 1994, the most recent. The Mott Foundation is also one of the earliest and largest private funders of the U.S. microenterprise movement. The original 1990 report surveyed twenty-one programs; that number had grown to thirty-one by 1994. Women's

1. Unfortunately, SELP data have not been released.

2. CfED is a national, nonprofit organization for economic development policy research, consulting, and demonstration projects. It concentrates on innovative enterprise development strategies that simultaneously expand opportunity and competitiveness. Maryland joined SEID in 1990 and is therefore not included in the studies cited here.

3. An additional report analyzing program costs is anticipated but has not yet been published.

4. Raheim and Alter (1995).

5. A total of 1,316 people participated in SEID; 408 of those, or 31 percent, started businesses during the time frame of the program. The evaluation is based on a telephone survey of 114 of these.

6. The design of the demonstration and the follow-up study also severely limit the generalizability of the findings. The authors of the evaluation acknowledge that SEID "did not permit random assignment. Individuals self-selected to participate in SEID. Consequently, findings from the demonstration cannot be generalized to the AFDC populations in participating states" (Raheim and Alter 1995, p. 3). In addition, SEID did not employ a control group, which makes it impossible to confirm the link between program participation and reported changes, such as exiting welfare.

7. The actual research and writing have been contracted out to the Corporation for Enterprise Development.

Initiative was included from the beginning. ISED and Accion New York were added in 1992 and Working Capital in 1994. The survey collected information on the financial status of each organization, its management practices or business strategies, the impact of each on individual customers or the community, and the issues each has faced in developing its program. The Mott studies focus on program data, although limited data on entrepreneurs were also collected.

The *Micro-Enterprise and Women* report was produced in 1994 by the Institute for Women's Policy Research (IWPR). Recognizing that microenterprise programs placed overwhelming emphasis on women and were heavily used by them, the IWPR conducted a study based on data from the Survey of Income and Program Participation, a national sample survey, in-depth interviews, and discussions of focus groups. The study "investigates the impact of self-employment and microenterprise as strategies to enhance the income package of AFDC recipients and other low-income women."[8] The goals of this study bear a striking resemblance to those of the SEID project: "to investigate whether there is a pool of current welfare recipients with self-employment experience and, if such a pool exists, to investigate their characteristics and the characteristics of their businesses"; and "to examine program changes and policy alternatives that could increase the use of microenterprises and the success of these enterprises as part of an income package."[9] However, the research design of the IWPR study is more sound than that of the SEID study, making its results more reliable.[10] During the period in which data were collected, very few microenterprise programs existed, so it is unlikely that the women included in this study had participated in microenterprise programs. Therefore, the study sheds little light on the effectiveness of such programs, although it does provide some very useful information on self-employment and the women who pursue it. The study focuses on women entrepreneurs and their businesses.

8. Spalter-Roth, Soto, and Zandniapour (1994, p. 3).
9. Spalter-Roth and others (1994, p. 14).
10. The primary target group of the IWPR study was women with some self-employment experience who receive means-tested transfer payments. In order to investigate the likelihood that this group can successfully pursue self-employment as an income-generating strategy, IWPR compared this target group (self-employed, current welfare recipients) with three other sample populations: self-employed, former welfare recipients; wage or salary packagers; and nonemployed welfare recipients (Spalter-Roth and others, 1994, p. 16).

Findings

The findings presented here draw from all four of the studies, as well as the work of other researchers. Findings are grouped in the categories of field, program, business, and entrepreneurs.

The Field

The number of programs, as well as activity within each, is expanding rapidly. Whereas a handful of programs was operating in 1990, by 1996 the Aspen Institute's *Directory of Microenterprise Programs* reported 328 programs, up from 195 in 1994 and 108 in 1992.[11] The numbers reflect only those programs that responded to a survey sent out by Aspen, so the actual numbers may be significantly higher. Early programs such as Women Venture (formerly WEDCO) and the Women's Self-Employment Project began to show solid achievement that attracted national attention among policymakers, organizers, and philanthropic foundations. Ninety-five percent of the programs offer technical assistance and training for entrepreneurs as of the 1996 directory; 73 percent do either individual or group lending. Of those that offer credit, 71 percent do individual lending only, 14.5 percent do group lending only, and the rest do both.

Growth in program activity expanded particularly rapidly between 1992 and 1994. The thirty-one programs surveyed by the Mott Foundation in 1994 reported a 35 percent increase in the cumulative volume of loans made and a 10 percent increase in the total capitalization of the loan funds in the previous two years. They also reported a 42 percent increase in the number of businesses financed.[12] Joyce Klein, who prepared the most recent Mott Foundation report, attributes the rapid expansion of the microenterprise field both to "growing need at the local and grassroots levels and increasing government interest at the state and federal levels."[13] According to Malcolm Bush of the Woodstock Institute, the "unbelievable" rate of expansion "speaks to the fact that there is a sector of economic problems we are not touching with regular economics."[14]

Microenterprise programs have begun to mature. The programs that have existed the longest, including most of those studied in this book,

---

11. Severens and Kays (1997).
12. Charles Stewart Mott Foundation (1994, p. 3).
13. Charles Stewart Mott Foundation (1994, p. 16).
14. Interview with Malcolm Bush, February 6, 1998.

are stable and have begun to diversify. They can envision their mission much more precisely and how they plan to fulfill it than they could even five years ago. This maturity has also created a cadre of people who have been working in the field for more than ten years and who have begun to conceive of and fill different needs. Some microenterprise programs have worked to create state-level organizations to do policy work, while others work with other organizations in regional alliances for economic development.

Another innovation is the development of state-level intermediaries. These organizations raise and leverage funds for microenterprise activity, taking some of the burden of fund-raising off the programs. The intermediaries also make decisions about the distribution of funding. Because the people involved in these organizations know the field, they are better equipped than most funders to determine where support should go. They also monitor programs that receive support so as to ensure proper accountability. Because the idea of the intermediary grew out of the field rather than the funding agencies, the theory is that intermediaries will be more likely to employ evaluation techniques and monitoring processes that programs can live with.

Practitioners have also started to develop means of evaluation. As programs matured, they increasingly saw the need, for themselves as well as for funders, to measure success. In 1997 the Aspen Institute, working directly with fifteen mature microenterprise programs, began MICROTEST, a major evaluation effort for the whole field. Recognizing the continued development and increasing diversity of the programs, leaders in the field are now seeking to clarify and define through appropriate performance measures what is meant by a high-quality microenterprise program. This effort is in its earliest stages, but six key areas for performance measures have been identified: reaching target groups, program scale, program costs and cost efficiency, program performance, program sustainability and internal cost recovery, and outcome and impact. MICROTEST's purpose is to establish a working group of microenterprise practitioners and researchers who will develop and test performance measures for the field. In the long run this endeavor should improve services by encouraging programs to measure performance regularly.

In general, microenterprise programs know more than outsiders do about what sorts of results they are producing, how to get money from funders, and how they should be evaluated. At the same time, the field is diversifying, as is discussed later.

The Programs

Microenterprise programs respond to their economic context. One aspect of this responsiveness has to do with recognizing and working with the skills of the target population. Programs that operate in an area with people who have few skills are likely to spend more resources on training than programs in which the target population has greater skills. This is particularly true of inner-city programs and those whose clients have depended on public assistance for a long time, such as Accion, WHEDCO, and ISED. In Lawrence, Massachusetts, Working Capital must recognize and work within the context of the Dominican culture in which most of its entrepreneurs operate. These people tend to be very entrepreneurial but must learn about operating a business in the United States. Likewise, programs that operate in remote rural areas must focus on the difficulty of access to markets, which is usually not an issue in more urban areas. Programs also continue to respond to changes in the economic and political landscape. Many, for instance, have created innovative responses to welfare reform: ISED is developing a program that would link potential employers with welfare recipients who have gone through the ISED program but are not ready for self-employment.

Microenterprise programs are learning organizations. The microenterprise strategy is new in the United States, and programs are continuing to climb a steep learning curve. In its 1993 update, the Mott Foundation found that 61 percent of the programs surveyed have changed their lending standards since they began.[15] The changes may involve implementing stricter, more banklike procedures; adding peer lending; requiring participants to borrow in steps from smaller to larger loans; or narrowing or expanding the target market.

In some areas there are clear trends among programs. Most notably, programs have increased their focus on collecting and evaluating data, often at the behest of funders. In other areas there are no clear trends in changes programs make. Some programs started with peer lending but have dropped it; others have recently added peer lending to the kinds of loans they offer.

Programs are also increasing the financing options they offer their clients and the noncredit services they provide.[16] Working Capital Lawrence

---

15. Charles Stewart Mott Foundation (1993, p. 5).
16. Klein (1994, p. 7).

recently formed a partnership with seven Massachusetts banks to provide larger loans to customers who are ready to borrow greater amounts than the program currently allows.

The numbers of changes that programs are introducing implies that it may be several years before the true potential of the strategy can be gauged. In many ways, studying microenterprise programs is like shooting at a moving target. Even the most mature programs continue to grow, experiment, and change. I would sometimes call programs several months after conducting fieldwork to ask for clarification on one aspect or another of the program only to learn from staff that they were making changes, sometimes in part because of conversations we had had during my time there.

Programs are extremely diverse. This diversity comprehends size, mission, type of lending, and target population. The most recent Mott Foundation update contrasts one program established in 1987 that has made more than 800 loans for $1.39 million with another established in 1986 that has made 241 loans for $345,000.

The diversity within and across programs reflects the diversity of their goals. Even though the basic goal of providing credit and training to entrepreneurs holds across programs, the emphases vary from improving self-esteem to alleviating poverty to more traditional economic development goals of creating jobs and expanding business. A 1994 study based on SELP findings attributes the diversity to differences in three aspects of the programs: their mission and anticipated outcomes, target population, and methodology.[17]

If classified according to their mission and anticipated outcomes, programs fall into two types: those that use microenterprise as a human development strategy and those that use it as a method of providing business development services. Differences in target population are discussed later. Differences in methodology help define three types of programs: credit-led individual programs, training-led programs, and group-lending programs.[18] Although they provide a useful framework, these categories are not mutually exclusive. For example, Working Capital is a credit-led group-lending program.

This diversity makes generalization difficult. The range of program types also speaks to the useful flexibility of the general strategy. It should, however, serve as a warning that all programs are not equal and should not be

17. Klein (1994, p. 3)
18. Klein (1994, p. 4).

judged by the same standards. Microenterprise program evaluation is evolving as the strategy itself continues to evolve. An appreciation of the malleability and resulting variety of program types will have to be built into evaluation.

Most programs do some form of targeting or directed outreach. Although nearly all microenterprise programs gear their services to low-income entrepreneurs, most also target or emphasize serving specific populations ranging from women (the most common) to displaced workers to migrant farm workers.[19] Programs target specific populations in order to respond to structural problems that make it difficult for certain groups to gain access to employment in the formal economy and to resources such as credit and training. This strategy also helps counteract regional employment problems, say, among timber workers or displaced homemakers. Many incorporate other kinds of assistance relevant to their target population into the basic business training. The Lakota Fund, for example, helps participants cope with alcoholism on their reservation. Accion New York assists borrowers with immigration and legalization problems.

Peggy Clark and Amy Kays, authors of the most recent SELP report, maintain that effective targeting makes for more client-effective programs. Arguing that U.S. programs require measures of success that go beyond the size and scale indicators often applied to LDC programs, they assert that the success of U.S. programs will depend in part on how well they can create and use "client-effective" service delivery mechanisms. Client-effective programs, they contend, will have strong links to communities, a close knowledge of microentrepreneurs and the economy in which they operate, and the ability to tailor particular services (training, technical assistance, and loans) to specific target groups on the basis of their needs.[20]

Serving microentrepreneurs—through training and lending—is expensive. SELP figures for 1994 indicate that the cost per client served ranges from $941 to $1,998.[21] ISED's cost per welfare client was $2,535 and for Women Venture's SETO Program $6,487.[22] The cost for each assisted busi-

19. The Aspen Institute's ongoing Self-Employment Learning Project is tracking 405 entrepreneurs from seven programs over five years. While seven is a small and not completely representative sample, 79 percent of the 405 entrepreneurs followed are women.

20. Clark and Kays (1995, p. 4).

21. Edgcomb, Klein, and Clark (1996, p. 34). These costs are the ratio of total self-employment program costs to the total number of clients served.

22. Edgcomb, Klein, and Clark (1996, p. 43).

ness (total program costs divided by the number of businesses in which clients are engaged) ranges from $1,759 to $9,033.[23]

The cost per loan in a 1996 SELP study averaged $1.47 per dollar loaned in 1994. Thus it cost the SELP programs between $1,688 and $15,329 for each loan made in 1994. On the surface this lending activity seems very expensive. The programs studied for the Mott Foundation evaluation showed an average cost per loan of $10,521.[24] The high costs occur, first, because the average loan in most programs is extremely small: $3,034 for Mott-funded programs.[25] So even though most microenterprise programs use market interest rates, the return is very low.[26] At the same time, the amount of paperwork is at least as great as for larger loans. And where many commercial banks have begun to automate their services, approving loans over the telephone, for example, microenterprise programs depend on forming strong relationships between lenders and borrowers to achieve low default rates. Creating and maintaining these relationships takes time, which costs money. In addition, virtually all microenterprise programs provide training as well as loans because many poor entrepreneurs are not ready to borrow as soon as they walk in. A recent study by Mt. Auburn Associates found that "successful group lending models tend to have lower costs than the individual models because of higher repayment rates and less staff time required per borrower, but the costs remain high, and even those programs that charge market interest rates and boast enviable repayment records require subsidies."[27]

Delinquency and default rates are higher than originally anticipated. Problems with early evaluation efforts coupled with high expectations generated by the experiences of programs in developing countries suggested that delinquency and default rates would be relatively low. However, 1993 data from the Mott Seed Capital Assessment showed an overall delinquency rate of 19.2 percent (using a portfolio risk measure) and an annual default rate of 9.5 percent.[28] The variation from program to pro-

23. Edgcomb, Klein, and Clark (1996, p. 37).

24. Charles Stewart Mott Foundation (1994, p. 8).

25. Charles Stewart Mott Foundation (1994, p. 5). Average loan sizes range from $300 to almost $12,000.

26. The range of interest rates charged is quite broad, however. Interest rates of the seven programs included in the SELP study range from 6.25 percent to 14 percent (Clark and Kays, 1995, p. 5).

27. Mt. Auburn Associates (1994, pp. 2–12).

28. Charles Stewart Mott Foundation (1994, p. 6).

gram is broad, however, and depends on such factors as types of businesses served (start-up or existing) and lending model employed. Mott Foundation research has also shown that default rates have gradually risen and that older programs generally have higher rates. Joyce Klein, author of the most recent foundation update, explains: "First, as programs mature and adopt stricter portfolio management practices, they typically become more aggressive about writing off bad loans. Second, programs that are more established tend to have a higher percentage of older loans [that] will have higher default rates simply because it takes time for a loan to go into default."[29]

Microenterprise programs have little trouble raising capital for their loan funds, but covering operating costs (which include training) continues to be a struggle. Funders, particularly public funders, like to think of microenterprise programs as low-cost ways of helping the poor. Because they provide loans, the implication is that the funds can be repaid. The connection between credit and opening a business is stronger in peoples' minds than the connection between training and entrepreneurship. According to Awilda Marquez, a board member at Women Entrepreneurs of Baltimore, "Policymakers and funders need to recognize that a training process is slower than credit. And we believe that it is more durable and longer lasting, that it is not a creamed program." Barbara Johnson, executive director of San Francisco–based Women's Initiative for Self Employment claims that "no one is willing to invest in the hard stuff. Credit is easy."

The 1994 Mott Foundation update found that, on average, microenterprise programs cover only 5.9 percent of their operating budgets through revenues from internally generated sources, including program revenue and investment income.[30] The remainder must be raised from public and private sources. No program anticipates being able to continue to pursue its mission and cover these costs.

Virtually all programs provide training as well as lending. Some programs such as ISED and WHEDCO do no lending. Of those that lend, nearly all require borrowers to undergo some basic business training encompassing sales, marketing, and finance, and many require would-be entrepreneurs to write a business plan. The distinguishing characteristic of programs is whether or not they provide access to credit, but it is far from the most important thing they do. The attention to programs as

29. Charles Stewart Mott Foundation (1994, p. 6).
30. Charles Stewart Mott Foundation (1994, p. 6).

banks, however, has stuck in part because funders, policymakers, and potential clients are all attracted by this aspect of them. The focus on credit is apparent, not actual; access to credit is a foil for other goals. The term *microcredit program* is something of a misnomer. Many loan funds have been started and funded on the assumption that lack of access to credit is the biggest barrier for poor people who want to become self-employed. But these potential entrepreneurs often come to microenterprise programs needing much more than credit. As a result, many programs have refocused their activities on a broader range of services, although they continue to differ from program to program. In some, including Women's Initiative, ISED, and Working Capital, a deemphasis on credit has always been an explicit part of their agendas. Others have shifted emphasis from credit access as staff have learned more about potential borrowers' full needs.

The combination of credit and training that microenterprise programs provide implies that these programs have learned from the SBA economic opportunity loans (EOLs) program of the 1960s, discussed in chapter 2, which did not prepare borrowers for business ownership. A 1991 report by the Mott Foundation found that programs spent between $110 and $2,000 per client on technical assistance.[31] This variation in costs reflects differences in the quantity and quality of training. Women's Initiative borrowers and ISED graduates must complete fourteen weeks of formal classroom training. At Working Capital, all training occurs informally within groups. According to SELP data, programs allocated between 21 and 88 percent of their total budgets to training activities in 1994.[32] Overall, 75 percent provide workshops, 33 percent provide mentors, and 66 percent do classroom training.[33]

As they mature, many programs are emphasizing training at least as much as lending. Jack Litzenberg, a funder with the Mott Foundation, which has supported microenterprise programs in the United States from the beginning, believes that in the wake of experience "microenterprise has not become a capital access strategy, it has become a community education program. [Programs] provide an entry point into understanding how the economy works. They learn by doing, they experiment with money, with buying and selling."[34]

31. Charles Stewart Mott Foundation (1994, p. 4).
32. Edgcomb, Klein, and Clark (1996, p. 33).
33. Charles Stewart Mott Foundation (1994, p. 5).
34. Interview with Jack Litzenberg, February 1998.

Microenterprise programs often give rise to networks of social service providers and community groups. In addition to business training and credit, low-income entrepreneurs need other social and professional services, such as child care and legal advice. This constellation of needs related to business ownership has moved many microenterprise providers to generate cooperation and collaboration within a community. Programs are formalizing this cooperation by creating partnerships, affiliates, and consortia to achieve scale and reduce direct costs.[35] Because most U.S. programs were initiated at the local level, they recognize and build on local institutions. Working Capital works with community development organizations to deliver its services and obtains most of its loan capital from area banks. ISED has a strong relationship with the Iowa Department of Human Services, through which it connects with welfare recipients. Programs with connections to community organizations and public agencies also have the added advantage of targeted access to potential borrowers.[36]

The contribution these programs make to community development—connecting people to each other and to critical organizations, training residents, and helping them gain access to resources—is often overlooked, perhaps because this aspect of their work is more difficult to see and evaluate. This work builds social capital, making microenterprise programs important facets in community development.[37]

Scale and sustainability are two of the biggest problems for microenterprise programs. In the face of small loans and high operating costs, many programs find it difficult if not impossible to process enough loans to achieve sustainability. Respondents to the Mott survey estimate that on average nearly 88 percent of their operating budgets will need to be generated from external sources; at present 94 percent of program budgets come from these sources. Credit-intensive programs are more likely to approach self-sufficiency than training-intensive programs because the former have lower operating costs and higher levels of revenue. Nearly all programs will continue to depend on external funding. They will therefore need to forge long-term commitments from funders, both public and private. The growing demand for the services provided by microenterprise programs requires a commensurate investment in them by the institutions

35. Klein (1994, p. 8).
36. Mt. Auburn Associates (1994, pp. 2–13).
37. Servon (1998b).

that currently use and support them. At the same time, it is important to recognize that programs vary in their pursuit of size. Some, like Women's Initiative, are more interested in empowering women to make sound economic life choices than in making a lot of loans, whereas Working Capital is expanding aggressively and one of the goals is to approach self-sufficiency. Clark and Kays make the case that scale and sustainability are appropriate measures of success in less developed countries but that U.S. programs require different measures.[38] These may include the ability of programs to graduate clients to the formal banking sector, to deliver cost-effective technical assistance and training, and to find cost-effective and client-effective service delivery mechanisms.[39]

Some programs have begun to emphasize efficiency and sustainable funding rather than self-sufficiency. According to Christopher Sikes of the Western Massachusetts Development Fund, "Even if you look at microenterprise development as a contained program, it will never be self-sustaining. Especially if it's a poverty program. It's more important to focus on efficiency and impact than on sustainability."[40] Welthy Soni, who runs the microenterprise program Business Start in Virginia, asserts that many funders

> expected these programs to be sustainable after a few years. Banks don't get to be sustainable until they have a lot of assets. To be sustainable with such a small portfolio is almost impossible. You can decide not to serve the hard-to-serve clients. You can work higher up the socioeconomic scale and serve less expensive clients, but many programs do not want to do that.

Other programs have begun to pursue tangential activities to generate income. Soni's program has diversified its loan portfolio. Although the primary focus is the microenterprise fund (which has $1 million lent out and another $1 million available to lend), the program has created another larger fund, using state money, targeted toward tourist activities and therefore also forwarding its mission of promoting local economic development.

Programs obtain funding from a mix of sources. Many sources specify whether funds are to be used for operating activities or lending. Mott Foundation data show that foundations contribute the largest share of

38. Clark and Kays (1995).
39. Clark and Kays (1995, pp. 3–4).
40. Interview with Christopher Sikes, February 1998.

program loan funds, 42 percent. Other contributors are the federal government, at 24 percent; state governments, at 19 percent; and various local and intermediary sources. Foundations also make the largest contributions to operating activities, 42.7 percent of the total. The federal government contributes 29.5 percent, state government 11.4 percent, and local government 2 percent.[41] The mix of funding has changed as policy has changed and as the popularity of microenterprise programs has grown.

The Businesses

Most microbusinesses are home-based sole proprietorships operating in the service sector, and most are less than five years old. Home-based business allows the entrepreneur to combine managing a business with child care, formal wage labor, and other responsibilities. Fifty-three percent of the businesses of self-employed former welfare recipients and an even higher percentage of the businesses of current welfare recipients provide services. Service businesses require little start-up capital and gain relatively easy entry into the market; and they require little in the way of overhead, equipment, and space. As in all self-employment, service businesses are labor intensive. Twenty-nine percent of the microentrepreneurs surveyed for the SELP study report working more than sixty hours a week, and 58 percent of these devote between 76 and 100 percent of their time to their business.[42]

Self-employment by itself does not sustain most microentrepreneurs' households. Slightly less than half of the entrepreneurs SELP interviewed reported making a profit in an average month.[43] Of the ninety-six SEID participants with businesses that were still operating when the survey was conducted in 1993, the median gross income was $8,000, and the mean net income was $4,446. Twenty-six business owners reported taking an owner's draw with a mean value of $574 a month, and eight reported paying themselves a regular wage with a mean value of $798. The IWPR study found that the businesses of self-employed former welfare recipients paid an average hourly wage of $4.38, while self-employed current welfare recipients made only $2.63. These same former recipients earned average hourly wages of $6.98 for wage or salary employment, while current recipients earned $4.00.

41. Charles Stewart Mott Foundation (1994, p. 6).
42. Clark and Kays (1995, p. 20).
43. Clark and Kays (1995, p. 28).

Furthermore, microbusinesses generally do not provide health insurance and child care. Only 6 percent of the businesses surveyed for SELP provided health insurance. The IWPR study found that self-employed former welfare recipients were covered by health insurance an average of only 2.5 out of 12 months, which was far less than the other groups studied. Given the lack of health insurance among these "successes," the authors concluded that "without universal health care benefits, self-employment is risky for women and their families."[44]

More than half (56 percent) of those surveyed by SELP claimed that their business provided them with their primary source of income.[45] Many microentrepreneurs do some form of income packaging. Sixteen percent of SELP participants received public assistance as a primary or secondary income source.[46] Thirty-seven percent of the sample reported holding down at least one job while running their businesses. These findings are complemented by results of the IWPR study:

> Welfare recipients who reported self-employment hours include this income source as part of a more diverse income package that includes wage or salary employment as well as other sources of income. These recipients had at least one business plus 1.4 wage or salary jobs for a total of 2.4 "jobs," on average, during a 24-month period. . . . Even "successful" former welfare recipients continue to be packagers of self-employment with wage or salary work. This is due to the fact that neither their businesses nor their jobs provide ample income to support families.[47]

The fact that wage labor does not adequately provide for many families' needs reflects the persistent phenomenon of working poverty. Because many current jobs offer only temporary or part-time employment, some entrepreneurs may vary the energy they put into their business depending on the other opportunities available to them at a particular time. But microentrepreneurs may retain formal wage labor to ensure adequate income while their business is stabilizing. However, the IWPR study found that "hourly earnings from self-employment are substantially lower than hourly earnings from wage or salary work . . . [suggesting] that wage or

44. Spalter-Roth and others (1994, p. 35).
45. Clark and Kays (1995, p. 20).
46. Clark and Kays (1995, p. 5).
47. Spalter-Roth and others (1994, p. 24).

salary work is a better financial option, if such work can be obtained steadily."[48]

These figures portray businesses that are hardly adequate to sustain households. As a result, nearly all microentrepreneurs are income packagers. Roberta Spalter-Roth and her colleagues define income packaging as combining paid employment, receipt of means-tested welfare benefits, and income from additional sources.[49] According to IWPR research, "Those women who combined work and welfare were more likely to bring their families out of poverty than those who did not; and they were also more likely to have health care for their families than those who cycled off welfare to low-wage jobs."[50] The researchers concluded that self-employment is probably "not, by itself, a likely means for bringing about the self-sufficiency of poor women, but it could be a part of an income package for a motivated group of AFDC recipients if certain public policies are changed."[51]

Critics of the microenterprise strategy often claim that self-employment provides the opportunity for a lateral move but fails to help people gain access to the mainstream economy. However, it may take several years for a business to become established and provide its owner with a living wage. This stabilization process is a fact of life for all small business owners and should not be used to argue against the usefulness of the microenterprise strategy. At the same time, self-employment may not be suitable for everyone, particularly the most vulnerable, who could lose their safety net.

Microenterprises create few jobs. Aside from the owner-operator, the 386 SELP businesses created 332 additional jobs. Sixty-six percent employed only the owner. Businesses involved in SEID created an average of half a job. Neither of these studies differentiates between full-time, part-time, and seasonal jobs. The sectors responsible for most job creation are restaurants, custodial firms, retail sales, and manufacturing.[52]

None of the studies examines potential causes for the small size of the businesses, but the potential reasons are fairly clear. Most microenterprises are less than five years old and are therefore in the start-up or stabilization phases rather than the expansion phases. Some microentrepreneurs are not interested in seeing their businesses grow; they would rather maintain

48. Spalter-Roth and others (1994, pp. 23–24).
49. Spalter-Roth and others (1994, p. 3).
50. Spalter-Roth and others (1994, p. 4).
51. Spalter-Roth and others (1994, p. 5).
52. Clark and Kays (1995, p. 26).

them at a manageable level. Women's businesses in particular are often criticized for failing to grow in the same way or at the same rate as men's businesses. According to Irene Tinker:

> For economists who consider profit making and growth the very essence of entrepreneurship, alternative behavior is dismissed as pre-entrepreneurial . . . the problem lies with the dominant economic value system, not the microentrepreneurs; the solution is for a paradigm shift to a more human economy.[53]

The concept of human economy acknowledges the legitimacy of valuing people and community welfare over the individual or self. It builds on data that show women continuing to "invest in their children's food or education [rather than investing in their businesses] despite accusations that this is not rational economic behavior."[54] Indeed, many of the entrepreneurs interviewed had made conscious decisions not to let their businesses grow beyond a certain point. Some preferred to pursue other interests or spend time with their families. Others wanted to focus on the activity that led to their self-employment in the first place; they did not want to become managers.

The Entrepreneurs

Microentrepreneurs need more than just credit. The most obvious things lacking among the people microenterprise programs serve are access to credit and business training. Both theorists and program practitioners have recognized these needs for years. Research has begun to document this claim from the point of view of entrepreneurs and potential entrepreneurs among the poor. Those interviewed for the SELP study ranked lack of capital and lack of business knowledge and skills as the top two barriers they faced to becoming self-employed. At the same time, there are many less obvious, but perhaps equally important, factors that also separate disenfranchised entrepreneurs from those who are better off. Participants in the SELP study said that support from relatives, education, and training all encouraged self-employment. Other influences included personal and professional networks that middle- and upper-class entrepreneurs commonly use to reach potential suppliers and buyers and to supply start-up

53. Tinker (n.d.).
54. Tinker (n.d.).

and expansion capital for their businesses. Wealthier entrepreneurs are also more likely to have access to child care, health care, and other necessary social services. Consistent with this, the IWPR study found that self-employed current welfare recipients are most likely to match the successes of self-employed former welfare recipients if they "receive additional training, access to financial and educational resources, and work more hours."[55]

Microentrepreneurs come from across the socioeconomic spectrum. The microenterprise strategy was imported to the United States as a way to serve potential entrepreneurs among the poor, in part because these are the people served in the developing world. But research has shown that programs serve far more than the poor. According to the SELP data for 1992, 42 percent of program participants earn less than $18,000 a year, but 15 percent earn more than $30,000. The median annual income is $29,054.[56] Although individual programs vary widely depending on their missions and target markets, the breadth of this range indicates that income is not the only factor impeding access to credit and training. It also implies that client pools within any given program are very diverse and therefore difficult to serve uniformly, and that income is a tricky measure to use to gauge a population's need for assistance. The income data reported by SELP do not take household size into account, nor do they distinguish between households in which the entrepreneur is the only earner and households with another earner present.

Survey data can only provide a snapshot, whereas longitudinal studies that track over time are much more telling. The SELP study is longitudinal and will look at changes once it is completed. Other questions that need to be addressed include: Does current low income reflect chronic poverty, or has the potential entrepreneur left a lucrative position to pursue a dream of self-employment? If an entrepreneur's income falls after moving from wage labor to self-employment, does this indicate failure or is the person actually happier, spending more time with family, participating in the community? Does a drop in profits reflect inadequate business training or a downturn in the economy?

Microentrepreneurs do not fit the underclass stereotype. Although many program participants have low incomes, the typical microentrepreneur is a skilled worker who pursues self-employment to increase income or improve life. Microentrepreneurs are relatively well educated. Eighty-three

55. Spalter-Roth and others (1994, p. 35).
56. Clark and Kays (1995, pp. 22–23).

percent of SELP participants have a high school education or more, with 39 percent having some college or a technical degree, 24 percent a college degree, and 9 percent some postgraduate work.[57] Sixty percent of SEID respondents had previous experience related to their business.[58] In the current economy, *some* college education no longer translates reliably into a stable, well-paying job with benefits that can sustain a family. This suggests what might be expected about any population of entrepreneurs: self-employment is serious business and requires time, skills, experience, and some kind of financial safety net.

Nearly half of all SELP respondents own their homes, and 63 percent of households have three or fewer members. Sixty percent of microentrepreneurs surveyed have no children under the age of twelve living with them.[59] To complete the profile, 62 percent are from a minority ethnic group, 78 percent are women, and more than two-thirds are between the ages of thirty and forty-nine.

These findings do not imply that the microenterprise strategy is failing, but they do suggest the kind of person who is best equipped to choose self-employment. Interviews with borrowers in the five programs I studied support SELP findings. The participants in these programs are at the least highly motivated; they are also often relatively well educated, experienced in their business, and have a support network of family and friends that provides them with a kind of safety net. The microenterprise strategy is generally targeted toward disenfranchised populations, but it is not geared to attracting "victims." Instead, it attracts and makes visible potential community leaders, people in a position to use the programs to help themselves and their businesses.

Self-employment is clearly best suited to a very specific population that includes some persistent poor but does not encompass all of them. Microenterprise programs *are* helping poor people, but most participants do not fit the underclass stereotype that tends to attract the lion's share of the attention in the media and in Washington. Although many microenterprise programs set out to bring entrepreneurship to the most disadvantaged populations, the course they have taken makes sense, given the demands of running a business. Perhaps the question should not be whether programs are serving the market they set out to serve but whether

57. Clark and Kays (1995, p. 17).
58. Raheim and Alter (1995, p. 33).
59. Clark and Kays (1995).

gaps in access to credit and training exist much higher on the socioeconomic scale than was expected. Skilled, educated people are not being served by traditional financial institutions. Forty-six percent of SELP respondents attempted to obtain business loans from other institutions; of these, 53 percent were denied credit. This finding does not imply that the microenterprise strategy is failing, but it does suggest which population is best equipped to choose self-employment.

Most microentrepreneurs are women. Seventy-eight percent of SELP participants are women. Although many programs specifically target women, those that do not often find that most of their clients are women. Interestingly, women are also the primary users of LDC-based programs. This implies that mainstream economic, financial, and educational institutions do not adequately meet women's needs. More and more women are being charged with ensuring the economic and social stability of households, and they require more options to help them succeed. That they are turning to microenterprise programs is evidence of their willingness to experiment with alternative ways of achieving self-sufficiency.

Recent demographic, economic, and social changes often require that women provide for the entire range of a family's needs and must find new ways to do so.[60] This phenomenon—the feminization of poverty—is generally understood to have placed women in a double bind of sorts, trying to fulfill both economic and household duties. Shifts in the structure of the global economy, the increasing number of female-headed households, and the continued segregation of available jobs have changed women's position both in relation to the household and to the larger economy.[61]

People pursue self-employment for two reasons. The SELP study found that 53 percent of respondents sought self-employment because they needed more money or were unemployed. These people may have considered self-employment not as a real choice but as their only economic option. Others generally possessed a skill or love for a particular activity from which they could start a business. Twenty-eight percent reported that "they started their business because they love what they do, they have the skills, and because they saw a market opportunity or community need that they thought they could fill."[62] Thus there seem to be two categories of people who pursue self-employment. True entrepreneurs always prefer to work

60. Pearce (1990); Garfinkel and McLanahan (1994); Spalter-Roth and others (1994).
61. Hartmann (1987).
62. Clark and Huston (1993, p. 7).

for themselves even if this does not appear to be an economically rational decision: they may work for lower wages and for longer hours in self-employment than they would in a wage job. Other entrepreneurs see self-employment as the best available option.

True entrepreneurs pursue self-employment because they do not seem to fit into the mainstream economy, often taking training in more than one area but unable to settle into a regular job. Before starting her daycare business, Grace had worked as a nurse's aide and had obtained her cosmetology license. She continues to do hair for a couple of regular clients and in this way supplements her income from public assistance and from her business. Dwight decided to open his own machine shop after being unable to resolve conflicts with his former employer. Sangeetha and Dan had also both had conflicts with employers. Asked why they preferred self-employment to work in the formal economy, Dan said: "It's calling your own shots. You know, you do good work for someone else, show care and commitment, and they walk on you. Making them money and them showing no respect. I think entrepreneurial people really feel the shackles. This was our last shot." They, like other true entrepreneurs interviewed, also decided to pursue self-employment because they believed in their product and got great satisfaction out of making customers happy.

Entrepreneurs for whom self-employment was the best available option included those who would gladly work for wages if they could make enough to support their families and those whose life paths were interrupted by an unplanned pregnancy, a job layoff, the dissolution of a marriage. In Iowa, three of the entrepreneurs interviewed turned to self-employment after losing well-paid factory jobs. They did not consider low-wage work without benefits to be an option, largely because it did not pay enough to allow them to afford child care and did not provide medical benefits for their children. Self-employment offered more hope and opportunity. Angie, a single mother of three, lost her $10-an-hour job with a meat-packing company in a small, industrial Iowa city when the plant she worked in closed in 1986.

> I worked for awhile as a school associate but it wasn't enough to carry the load. I went on welfare and I had three kids at home at the time. I was in the middle of buying a house when the plant closed, and my bills got to the point where without a college degree I couldn't get a job that would support us, so it was kind of sink or swim. My kids' fathers were absent and I wasn't getting any child support.

Angie went through the ISED program and opened a consignment clothing store, which helped her leave welfare. Still struggling to make ends meet each month, she claims that she could not have made the transition without the waiver provided by the state that allowed her to continue receiving public assistance until her business stabilized. She also listed ISED and her mother, who had "been here from the word go," as factors that made her current self-sufficiency possible. Self-employment has enabled Angie and her family to survive without public assistance, but the road has been rough. She earns far less than she did at the plant, and her family has sacrificed a great deal. Asked what advice she would give someone who was in her shoes ten years ago, she said,

> I'd tell her to go to school, don't necessarily go into business. Your family makes more sacrifices this way than if you work a forty-hour week. It's nice to be self-employed but it's also nice to have a paid vacation. It takes more dedication to do this. I felt like self-employment was really my only option. If I could have gotten another job that paid well, I would have taken it.

Others pursue self-employment because of family situations. Jim, one of two single fathers interviewed for this study, has two daughters. After his wife abandoned the family, he left his job at a battery company because he could not spend the time required to make out-of-town deliveries and care for his daughters at the same time. In February 1995 he quit his job, went on public assistance, and began a television repair business in his basement. After working with ISED, he moved to a storefront. Having a business, he says, allows him to take better care of his children. He is closer to home and can get away more easily if one is sick. Jim has also relied on Iowa's waiver program, as well as crucial support from family and ISED.

Like true entrepreneurs, many of those who originally pursued self-employment because of an unplanned event claim that they much prefer self-employment to working for someone else. The advantages they cite include flexibility, control, pride in what they do, and freedom. The disadvantages include long hours, unreliable income, and the lack of benefits.

Most microentrepreneurs have strong support networks and are fiercely determined to succeed. For many entrepreneurs, self-employment more easily allows them to fulfill the household and economic obligations that single parents must meet. At the same time, those who have successfully made the transition from welfare to self-employment have the solid support of family and friends. Some microentrepreneurs interviewed have family members who watch their stores when they need to be elsewhere. Others have family and friends who help with financial planning and book-keeping. Many rely on parents, siblings, and friends to watch their children after school. Still others have received help from family and friends with renovations to their storefronts and donations of other necessities.

Microenterprise programs clearly add to and strengthen these networks. Many of the entrepreneurs interviewed spoke of the importance of the relationships they had forged with the business consultants and trainers at microenterprise programs. These relationships function to boost self-confidence and to get the entrepreneurs to a place that enables them seriously to pursue their businesses. Most of the successful entrepreneurs maintain these relationships after graduation and continue to use them as a resource to obtain access to information, funding, and other resources.

Conclusion

The picture that emerges from past research is one of a strategy that can be implemented in a variety of ways, serves a broad range of entrepreneurs, and achieves a diversity of outcomes. Thus far that research has been by and large descriptive; it therefore raises as many questions as it answers. These questions concern the more complex activities of programs, the people they serve, and the work that they do that extends beyond starting businesses. These questions can only be answered through a finer examination of the microenterprise strategy, which is what the rest of this book does.

FOUR   *Economic*
Development or
Social Welfare?

As THE PRECEDING chapters show, microenterprise programs defy simple classification into any predetermined policy or program category. They work toward both economic development and poverty alleviation. Economic development is generally concerned with job creation but usually on a much larger scale than microenterprise programs undertake. Poverty alleviation typically has to do with moving people off welfare and into the work force, and often focuses on reforming individual and family characteristics. Microenterprise programs do some of these things, too, but not in traditional ways. How and with what limitations they blend elements of both policy fields is the subject of this chapter.

Three microenterprise programs are examined in detail: Women's Initiative for Self Employment (Women's Initiative) in San Francisco–Oakland, which serves low- and moderate-income women; Working Capital in Boston, which targets specific communities but not individual characteristics; and Accion New York, which is based in Brooklyn and targets Latinos. The three programs present an interesting range of ways in which microenterprise programs balance their economic development and poverty alleviation work.

Fieldwork shows that these programs marry the traditional objectives of economic development and poverty alleviation in the access to credit they provide and the outcomes they achieve. Because they fail to fit neatly into either policy sphere, however, traditional evaluation techniques are unable to rate their performance adequately.

Microenterprise Development as Economic Development

Economic development means improving the economic health of a region. Economic development programs and policies strive to accomplish this by supporting the generation, stabilization, expansion, and attraction of businesses to a particular area. Typical economic development strategies include tax abatements, subsidies, and low-interest loans to businesses. Microenterprise programs work within the economic development sphere because they provide loans and training geared to creating and expanding business. The target population of most programs has no other access to these critical resources. Therefore the programs function to create a new class of entrepreneurs and businesses that most likely would not exist otherwise. Microenterprise programs also contribute to economic development outcomes indirectly through the training and economic literacy skills they provide. Many of the program participants who do not go on to start businesses leave programs able to participate in the mainstream economy in ways that they could not before their involvement with microenterprise programs.

Microenterprise Development as Social Welfare

Social welfare programs use various mechanisms to lift low-income people above the poverty line. The emphasis of such programs has shifted dramatically in the past few years from welfare to workfare, in response to widespread dissatisfaction with Aid for Families with Dependent Children (AFDC), the program that historically constituted the cornerstone of the modern U.S. welfare state. Self-sufficiency, a central concern of workfare programs, is also the focus of microenterprise programs. Most microenterprise programs target low-income people. All help participants become self-sufficient, either through the creation of a business alone, through the extra income that a part-time business can generate to supplement other income, or through the acquisition of critical skills that provide greater access to the labor market. Microenterprise programs also enable participants to repair faulty credit histories, thereby providing them with more financial tools for attaining self-sufficiency.

Programs Studied

How does each program balance economic development and social welfare goals? A close look at the operations of each program shows that they all do it differently.

Women's Initiative for Self Employment

Women's Initiative was begun in 1986 by a group of women guided by a philosophy of equity and empowerment. They shared a strong belief in the capacity of women to be economically independent and in credit and training as a way to increase the economic options available to women.

The idea of starting a microenterprise program for women in the Bay Area came from Paulette Meyer, the current chair of the board of directors. Meyer was with the Levi Strauss Foundation in 1986 doing community development work when she learned of a Minneapolis-based microenterprise program for women called WEDCO.[1] Started in 1983 by Kathy Keeley, a woman whom Meyer and others have called "the mother of this movement" in the United States, WEDCO evolved into a template that Women's Initiative and many other programs followed. Meyer arranged to have Keeley speak to a group of funders in 1986 to drum up interest for a similar project in the Bay Area. The meeting resulted in a planning grant and a relationship with the San Francisco Women's Foundation, which sponsored Women's Initiative in its generative phase.

During this same period Barbara Johnson, the current executive director of Women's Initiative, conducted an analysis of services in the Bay Area and found that women at all socioeconomic levels were in sore need of financial services and capital assistance. Furthermore, they all faced similar issues, from "the lowest-income monolingual immigrant woman all the way to the higher-income corporate dropout women who were looking for similar kinds of services to start businesses." Some of the strategies that could be used to address these needs differed from one population to the next, but the needs themselves were similar. Johnson's study provided fuel for the argument that disenfranchisement from the financial world was not only a socioeconomic issue, it was also a gender issue.

Only low- and moderate-income women are eligible for Women's Initiative loans. Although this means that the Women's Initiative loan fund is used solely to fund the businesses of lower-income women, this category needs to be deconstructed. It includes women ranging from Dorothy, who depends on both welfare and the income generated from her meat delivery business to survive from month to month, to Alison and Liz, whose financial safety net includes family, friends, and their own ability to obtain

---

1. This program is currently called Women Venture. It has no relation to the WHEDCO program that was studied for this book.

individual credit through credit cards. Many clients are "poor" because they left a relationship that supported them, left a job that paid a living wage, or felt a need to assert their independence from the kind of control that often accompanies reliance on others for financial stability. Rather than judge how and why these women became poor, Women's Initiative trusts that their decisions were right for them. A goal of the program is to help them remain strong in these decisions. As Miriam Walden, a Women's Initiative business consultant and manager of the loan fund, has said,

> I think if we help people to be powerful in saying, 'Right now I want this and not a ten-dollar-an-hour job,' then the next time that they're faced with saying, 'No, now I don't want this anymore,' then they're still better off. But there's a whole group of people that we serve that maybe just want to do this because they can't find a ten-dollar-an-hour job. Women's Initiative is interested in helping women decide what their best available option is and then pursue it.

PHILOSOPHY. Although the Women's Initiative mission emphasizes neither training nor lending, it has been operationalized largely through training. Johnson claims that initially the idea was to provide women who thought they might want to start businesses with "very key resources and energy" that would enable them "to make informed decisions before they squandered their resources—energy and financial. . . . So really the lending program is only grease for the wheel." The wheel in this instance obviously increases women's economic options.

Two decisions made during the formative stages of Women's Initiative—to focus the mission on increasing women's economic options rather than on credit per se, and to serve only women, primarily lower-income women—have strongly affected the current shape of the program.[2] By keeping the mission broad and devoting program energy to the entrepreneur rather than the business or more traditional economic development outcomes, the program encourages two things to happen. First, the potential borrower brings to the table all kinds of other issues, which may or may not be directly related to the business. And second, the lender role expands to deal with these matters.

"Holism" is a word that came up repeatedly in interviews with borrowers, staff, and board members. Women's Initiative focuses on helping

---

2. Since this research was conducted, Women's Initiative has decided to serve only low-income women.

women make better-informed life decisions, a goal that requires a much broader approach than simply making as many loans as possible. In addition, several of those interviewed mused about whether the comfort level and holism they experienced at Women's Initiative resulted directly from the fact that it is a women's organization. Although no one could clearly articulate why they saw a link between gender and certain qualities throughout the institution, all borrowers remarked on the connection.

Field experts and Women's Initiative board and staff had more clearly defined explanations. Meyer believes that the holism stems from the assumption that credit is just one—and possibly the last—step on a much longer journey. On this topic, she states,

> Do we have credit problems? Yes. Do we need credit programs to address that? Yes. Is it the central element? I don't think so. I think it really takes a combination of lots of different services working with the lending component. . . . Once you've been able to create . . . a viable home situation and a viable person that has self-belief, confidence, money management skills, and everything else that [she needs] in place, then you have the opportunity to create a business that can succeed in achieving community economic development.

This attitude toward access to credit has had a tremendous effect on the configuration of the program. Rather than lending to entrepreneurs who are already ready to borrow, as many programs do, Women's Initiative has chosen to turn people into successful borrowers, which entails engaging in a much broader range of activity.

TARGETING WOMEN. Starting a program to help women came naturally to Women's Initiative's founding mothers. In addition to having worked on community development issues—Meyer was working in a community development program and Johnson was just finishing a degree in city and regional planning focusing on economic development when they launched the program—both had long histories of activism in the women's movement. Before studying city planning, Johnson went to business school to, as she puts it, "learn the skills that I really saw the women's movement needing." Using WEDCO as a successful example also helped them gain support for the idea of linking women and self-employment.

Many of the women I interviewed admitted to having problems with handling money, understanding economic matters, or working with numbers. They typically linked these to gender. Researchers in education have begun to study why girls do not perform as well in science and math as boys do after a certain age. One experimental solution to the problem, all-girl science and math classes, has shown impressive results. Several of the women I interviewed went to Women's Initiative for training because they thought they were "no good at numbers" and that Women's Initiative would provide a safe environment in which to learn. Lydia admitted, "I wouldn't have gone to their classes if it wasn't a woman-focused organization. . . . I know that for a fact. . . . I could almost feel like if I were to go to somebody else they would just laugh at me." Anne went to Women's Initiative "to do financial planning." "I'm not sure at that point that I knew I needed a loan," she says. "I think I was just so accustomed to being very poor and living from hand to mouth, which is still a bad habit that I have. . . . Just being able to get by from month to month, pay the rent, hold off the creditors."

Johnson and other Women's Initiative staffers told me that many of the women the program serves, particularly populations such as Latinas, fail to see their entrepreneurship as economic activity. Johnson explains that "a lot of loans are small [because] a lot of women have a hard time really identifying what they're doing as a business. They kind of look at it as 'in addition to' or they look at it as a sideline, or part time or something." The decision to borrow is itself a huge one for most women. According to Walden, "Most of the community of women that we interact with are people who come in only after having gone through a long process of self-debate about it. . . . And they're coming to you having really made up their minds that they want something and what they want it for." This cautious approach to borrowing is likely connected to the uneasiness that many women expressed regarding money and financial matters.

Many women linked their attitudes and behavior to gender when talking specifically about their business. Some talked of having trouble asking for a loan and of being uncomfortable with success. On this subject, Kate told me, "[Women] don't necessarily assume that they're going to succeed. I think men really do assume, one way or another, that that's their lot in life. Women have to grapple with that." Both Johnson and Walden said they thought women were less comfortable taking risks with money than men. Talking specifically about the borrowing process, Walden says, "The majority of women are much more conscious about borrowing and much more, kind of rational in their thinking . . . they haven't bought into the fantasy of the wealthy entrepreneur that much. . . . They don't have role models like that, and so they don't act like that."

Several of the women I interviewed also recognized that they had the bad habit of undervaluing their product or service. Julia described the problem as a difference in the way people perceive men and women:

> I don't think that women perceive men in that way, that I should just be accessible all the time. . . . And that's a problem I have in running my business, because I feel like I don't prioritize things very well, that I do make myself accessible. . . . Like for me, some choreographer will call and whine about how much rent costs, and I'll give them a break, and then later it dawns on me that I am subsidizing this person's work and I don't have enough money to do my own. . . . So I have to constantly remind myself of my priorities. . . . I think men's priorities . . . stay much more in the front of their brain. . . . And I think that when you do put your foot down, as a woman, say the buck stops here and draw some boundaries, people perceive you as a bitch.

According to Kate, "The women I know in business tend to give it away too much. Discounts—it's crazy. Erica [her business consultant] was always telling me to stop it, but I wouldn't. There's something wrong with us. We don't feel like we deserve to be successful."

This array of problems—lack of self-confidence, anxiety about finances, and discrimination in the corporate world and other mainstream institutions—provides strong support for Women's Initiative's decision to target women. As part of her explanation of why microenterprise programs overwhelmingly target, and are run by, women, Barbara Johnson said, "Women understand what women need, and women . . . have a tendency to make more comprehensive programs and not just the nuts and bolts, and get into the social issues, the psychological issues, dependency issues, all of those."

On a more general level the feminization of poverty coupled with recent changes in the welfare system has created a population of women who need new strategies to help them provide for themselves and their families. Chapter 5 includes a discussion of self-employment in the context of welfare reform. Intuitively, a program like Women's Initiative, which provides access to credit and technical assistance, makes sense as a way to help women cope with the changing context in which they must organize their lives. "The vision was really coming from very much of a feminist viewpoint," said Johnson. "That women's roles are complicated and women needed more options available to them, more economic options available to them. That it was not simply a matter of short-term training and budgeting. It was a much broader mandate of helping women to empower themselves."

THE PLACE OF WOMEN'S INITIATIVE ALONG THE ECONOMIC DEVELOPMENT–SOCIAL WELFARE CONTINUUM. Women's Initiative helps alleviate persistent poverty by singling out the group (low-income women) that is both most needy and, oftentimes, most prepared to help itself by using a strategy such as microenterprise. The support networks that operate in poor communities and often control the flow of resources tend to be maintained by women. These women support the churches, watch the streets, and care for the community's children.[3] Although they are among the most logical candidates for self-employment within the urban poor population, the magnitude and diversity of their other responsibilities, coupled with the immense energy required to run a business, make it difficult for many to meet conventional definitions of success with their businesses. Instead, many use self-employment as part of a larger survival strategy that may include receipt of public benefits and part-time or temporary work. Definitions of success must be broadened to include these women. Although they are not showing rapid movement up the socioeconomic ladder, they are better equipped to meet their needs as a result of participating in programs. Policy barriers pose additional problems for program participants on the lowest rungs of the socioeconomic ladder. And as the 1996 welfare reform legislation becomes institutionalized, self-employment may begin to loom larger in the patchwork financing that enables the women to get by from one month to the next.

Given that Women's Initiative works on increasing the individual economic empowerment of women and that nearly half of the clients currently served by the program have very low incomes, the program does help to combat the problem of persistent poverty. The increasing feminization of poverty and the fact that the majority of poor households are headed by women provide strong support for targeting women. Teaching them about the option of self-employment makes them more likely to be resilient when changes in the larger economy make it difficult to obtain stable, long-term employment that pays a living wage. At Women's Initiative, says Johnson, "the focus is on women changing their relationship to the market. Women have been acted upon by the market, have been reac-

3. Stack (1974).

tive to the market. In human and technical and personal development, what we say is that they become actors. And that is a very big change in personal identity." Self-employment also helps women engage in activity that simultaneously allows them to provide for and care for their children. At the same time, the women most in need of alternatives—poor, single mothers—are the ones who have the hardest time dealing with the demands of self-employment, according to research conducted by the Institute for Women's Policy Research.[4] This finding is supported to some extent by the research I present: many women leave the program before starting a business in order to get their lives to a place that allows for starting a business. Those who do ultimately borrow fare better if they have a strong network of family and friends to help them.

Whether Women's Initiative can be thought of as an economic development organization is a tricky question. The majority of board and staff I asked to comment on it gave a qualified yes and no. The affirmative part derives from the fact that Women's Initiative is helping some businesses to start, grow, and provide jobs both for their owners and for others. Most staff members hesitate to emphasize this component, however, because it is not what the program emphasizes. There is a widely held belief at Women's Initiative that what the program provides constitutes a necessary step that precedes and sometimes includes economic development but is broader and meets other needs. Paulette Meyer argues that "economic development" is a problem term because it excludes the need for services; at the same time, she recognizes that

> one of the reasons that everyone has focused on economic development as the solution is because it's more powerful, [but] sometimes our poverty population is poor for reasons that really have very little to do with the availability of jobs or economic development. . . . I think it's so important not to view this movement as a microcredit movement, but rather as a movement that is a more holistic approach to women's self-sufficiency.

In comparison with traditional economic development strategies, which focus on significant increases in jobs created, the businesses Women's Initiative helps, others point out, are too small to make a large contribution. This is not to say that what the program does is unimportant, but rather that it requires a more appropriate descriptor. According to Miriam Walden,

4. Spalter-Roth, Soto, and Zandniapour (1994).

"These businesses, economically, are not big and powerful. So naturally, they . . . don't have as much ability to generate jobs and do economic development. And so if what you wanted was economic development, you've picked the wrong horse to ride."

Clearly, Women's Initiative lies closer to the social welfare end of the continuum than to the economic development end. Given that the microenterprise strategy continues to be marketed and discussed in economic development circles and measured using economic development indicators, the program will have to continue its present efforts to document the broader range of outcomes it is producing, as well as to show how these results often ultimately lead to more conventional economic development.

Accion New York

Brooklyn-based Accion New York is a project of Accion International, which does development work throughout Latin America. Begun in July 1991, Accion New York serves the low-income Latino community in New York City by providing market-rate loans and basic business training to the self-employed. The program makes loans both to groups and to individuals.

Initially, Accion International was dedicated to the broad mission of fostering political and economic development in Latin America. It shifted its focus to individual businesses in 1973, at which time the organization began to provide credit and training to the self-employed poor. Over the next two decades Accion expanded its services to fourteen Latin American countries. In 1993 it provided more than $202 million in loans to 205,956 microentrepreneurs. The average loan size in Latin America is $100, and the majority of loans are made to women.[5] The payback rate is 98 percent.

Accion initiated its New York affiliate program in the Williamsburg section of Brooklyn in 1991 on the basis of a six-month feasibility study showing a similar lack of access to capital that Accion International worked to remedy in Latin America. The study found significant numbers of men and women pursuing self-employment to survive. Unable to obtain credit from traditional financial institutions or, in many cases, even from credit

5. The ratio of male to female clients has begun to equalize; in 1993 women represented 54 percent of Accion International's clients.

cards, they used loan sharks to finance their businesses. In 1990, 19.3 percent of all New Yorkers lived in poverty, 41 percent of all poor people were of Latino heritage, and close to 33 percent of the entire Latino population in New York was living in poverty.[6] Accion has since targeted areas in the United States where immigration has led to a high concentration of Latinos.

Although these conditions argue for the need for Accion's services, there are important differences between the U.S. and Latin American contexts. For one thing, the informal economy is much stronger and easier to access in Latin American countries than it is in the United States. For another, microenterprises in developing countries are much more highly concentrated than they are here. In addition, many undocumented immigrants fear asking for help because they are afraid of being deported. The amount of capital necessary to stabilize, expand, or formalize a small business in the United States is much higher than in the developing world: the average Accion International loan in Latin America is $100; in New York it is $2,328. Finally, working with Latinos in the United States is not the same as working with a uniform culture. Accion New York clients come from the entire range of countries and cultures in Central America, South America, and the Caribbean.[7]

In October 1990 Accion International hired Delma Soto to initiate the New York program. Although Soto was given a large measure of autonomy in starting the program, certain elements of the Accion International methodology were transferred. Unlike most U.S. microenterprise programs, for example, Accion does not work with start-up businesses. Rather than provide seed capital, Accion targets existing enterprises that require working capital. These generally need loans between $500 and $25,000 to stabilize or expand operations. In addition, all client participants are borrowers; there is no separate training component. Any training that takes place occurs informally through the credit component.

It took Soto about three months to set up an office and find an administrative assistant. She began to meet officially with other agencies, banks, and funders in January 1991. Soto continued to encounter problems with community groups that also serve Latinos because, she thinks, "they still viewed us as competition." In addition, the microenterprise concept was still relatively unknown in the United States in 1990, which may help

6. Cited in Acosta (1995, p. 4).
7. Acosta (1995); and Novogratz (1992).

explain why community-based organizations were initially reluctant to refer clients to Accion. Soto says that she tried to include these organizations because "the standard way that you implement any new program is that you work through existing community agencies. So that's what I was trying to do. But I didn't have that background. My background was an MBA, very commercial corporate America." She therefore abandoned her first strategy and went with what she knew. Her background in banking, she believes, enabled her to get the program off the ground.

One of Accion International's goals in launching a U.S. program was to learn whether its methodology of group lending would work in the U.S. context. Therefore Accion New York started out doing only group loans. Program administrators believed that if both group and individual loans were offered at the beginning, no one would want to participate in the group process. In its first nine months of promotional activities, Accion New York screened over 250 inquiries from men and women seeking loans for their businesses and began to disburse loans of $2,000 or less on July 30, 1991. Accion New York began making individual loans in 1992 at a point at which growth in group lending began to level off. Potential borrowers were experiencing difficulty forming groups, and many were able to provide the collateral and cosigner necessary to take out an individual loan. Interestingly, although the program has grown because it has incorporated individual lending, most borrowers who started out borrowing in groups have continued to do so. Sixty percent of loans are still group loans.

PHILOSOPHY. Three critical and somewhat interconnected decisions made early in the history of Accion New York are largely responsible for the current configuration of the program. They are the use of a commercial banking model, the virtual exclusion of training, and the decision not to serve start-ups. The Latino target market has not shaped the program to nearly the extent that serving women has shaped Women's Initiative. As a result of these early decisions, Accion New York carries out its mission almost solely through its credit activities.

Soto began the program using a commercial banking model combined with the Accion methodology, and this configuration has remained much the same. The orientation toward microlending distinguishes Accion New York from other programs. Soto recognizes this. Aside from the decisions to serve only existing businesses and to focus on credit rather than training, she believes that the biggest difference between Accion New York and other programs is that it is "very bottom-line driven. Every decision that's made is based on a business implication as opposed to a social. It's not the social aspect that's motivating us, it's the business side of it. The social aspect happens as a result of making the right business decisions." Indeed, many borrowers think of Accion New York as a bank that happens to care about its clients and establishes relationships with them. Most other microenterprise programs are more like community organizations or training programs that happen to make loans. Credit is the focus at Accion in a way that strongly differentiates it from other programs.

TARGETING LATINOS. In much of Latin America, self-employment is a common survival strategy. Discussing the success of microenterprise programs in developing countries, Jacqueline Novogratz has written that in the majority of these contexts "there is no welfare system that provides a safety net, nor is there the likelihood of securing comfortable wage-earning positions. In countries where the informal sector flourishes, microenterprises are a means to survive."[8] It makes sense that, upon arriving in the United States, many immigrants turn to self-employment as a way to get by. Many have relied on self-employment in their countries and have been raised in families that run small businesses. Novogratz maintains that "entrepreneurship is a multigenerational phenomenon."[9] Undocumented immigrants in particular cannot collect public assistance and generally face a difficult time obtaining work in the formal economy. Accion New York estimates that 20 percent of its borrowers are undocumented. According to Soto, the phase between arriving in this country and becoming documented is when they most need help.

> If you really want to help people, you have to help them in the situation that they're currently in, and if I'm only willing to work with them once they've got their businesses licensed and they're paying taxes, that's not when they need my help. They need my help to get to that point, and no one's going to work with them other than the loan sharks. So we have to do it.

Many Accion borrowers have advanced educations in their home countries and obtain a work permit upon arriving in the United States but do not possess the language skills to obtain work. Their options are extremely

8. Novogratz (1992, p. 9).
9. Novogratz (1992, p. 14).

limited if they are not fluent in English. Opening a business in a Latino neighborhood is a much more attractive route to most than working long hours for low pay and no benefits in a factory or in a low-level service sector job. Many immigrants also have dependents both in the United States and abroad. They may start a business that they can operate in the hours that they are not working at a regular job as a way of making extra money. Many therefore join the 10,000 unlicensed vendors in New York City.[10] Others sell product lines such as Amway and Avon door to door or produce food and clothing to supply the vendors.

Accion International decided to target Latinos in its New York affiliate because the organization already had expertise working with the Latino population and because programs like Accion are needed in the United States in view of all the barriers these immigrants face. According to Hector Cariño, a loan officer who has been with Accion since 1992, a combination of factors has led the program to focus on Latinos: "The language. Immigration laws a lot, being illegal in this country. Or not being able to use their knowledge, because they graduated from college . . . but they cannot use it because they do not have a social security number, things like that." Also, immigrant entrepreneurs are likely to need access to credit even more than their U.S.-born counterparts because they are less likely to have established support networks of family and friends who can afford to lend to them. Interestingly, the program has attracted few Puerto Rican clients. Cariño believes that this is primarily because they enjoy the benefits of U.S. citizenship. Freer access to the labor market and mainstream financial institutions makes them less likely to need self-employment as an option.

For most of the Latino population, lack of access to credit presents the biggest obstacle to pursuing self-employment. Offering small business credit in a Spanish-speaking setting, then, makes sense. Demand is concentrated; it is relatively easy to target Latinos in New York because they are generally clustered in particular neighborhoods and are reachable through the Latino media and community groups.[11] In addition to the language, Latinos are more likely to trust a Latino organization than a mainstream financial institution, particularly if they are undocumented. Several borrowers claimed that their friends and family had warned them not to go to Accion because the low interest rates were too good to be true. Many seem to

10. Accion estimate.
11. Acosta (1994).

believe either that the government is using the organization to obtain information or that it is a scam organized by people trying to take advantage of new immigrants. This skepticism has created problems for the organization in terms of outreach.[12]

Most of the people interviewed for this study were referred to Accion by former or current clients. Although they liked the fact that Accion is a Latino organization, they would have participated even if it did not target. For most borrowers the ideals of the organization are more important than its focus on Latinos. Rafael, a taxi driver, says his relationship with Accion would be the same even if "it was not Latino but it had the same principles on which it decided whether or not to make loans [I would still go]. . . . [What matters is] if a person is good or bad; it's not necessary that they be Latino." Mario echoed this sentiment:

> It's more important that it's a community organization, and that it has the mission of serving the community, of serving people who need to work. . . and who want, in one way or another, to establish their own business. . . . The people [at Accion] have the capacity to understand the problems of people with few resources who want to have a business. It doesn't matter that they're Latino.

At the same time, several borrowers appreciated the Latino focus because they said it allows the people at Accion to understand them better. Thelma, for one, said that Accion's Latino focus "has helped me because, one, they speak my language, and two, Latinos can help each other more."

Cariño claims that in terms of program operations the main result of targeting is that it is easier and quicker to establish relationships with borrowers and to discover whether they will be responsible borrowers. There appears to be little relationship between the decision to target Latinos and the way the program is configured. Soto believes that working within a Latino culture has not affected the program except in the way Accion does outreach. "In terms of marketing, yes," she says, "but not in terms of the operational aspects of it." This is a big difference from Women's Initiative, for example, where borrowers, staff, and board believe that the holistic nature of the program and its focus on women are inextricably linked.

---

12. In her recent marketing plan for Accion, Acosta writes that for the program "to reach informal sector entrepreneurs, Accion's outreach material must address their fear of reprisal from tax, licensing, and other government agencies" (1995, pp. 31–32).

ACCION AND THE ECONOMIC DEVELOPMENT–SOCIAL WELFARE CONTINUUM. Accion New York provides credit to make self-employed people and their businesses more productive. Given that a significant number of borrowers have experienced increases in income as a result of borrowing at Accion, the program is helping some Latinos stay out of poverty and stabilize their businesses. To a greater extent than in the other programs, the target population at Accion has limited options. Many are immigrants who must pursue self-employment to survive. Entrepreneurs in other programs may have other jobs or can depend on a partner with a more stable job (and the benefits that go along with it), but the Accion borrower is often the household breadwinner.

Like most microenterprise programs, Accion New York operates on too small a scale to make a substantial contribution to economic development. The program serves a niche in the market by providing a product to which its target population has no other access. According to Hector Cariño, "We are giving the opportunity to somebody to do something that otherwise it would be really difficult to do, being here [in this country]. Because we have clients that in their country it was a completely different story how their life was before. But being here there was no way they could do something like that . . . without a program like this." Accion New York is the closest thing to a purely alternative credit institution that exists in the U.S. microlending world. It approaches what it does like a business that is filling an unserved need rather than as a social organization attempting to rectify an inequity.

Working Capital, Cambridge, Massachusetts

Working Capital launched its first operations in rural New Hampshire in September 1990. Since then the program has spread, serving areas of Maine, Vermont, New Hampshire, Massachusetts, Florida, and Delaware. The program expanded into the Boston area in 1992; I look only at Working Capital's Boston project. All training and lending takes place within a peer group structure. The program was designed to serve low-income persons and economically distressed communities but does not exclude anyone from participating.

Working Capital embodies the vision of founder Jeffrey Ashe. Ashe learned about the microenterprise strategy firsthand in its international context. He worked for Accion International for twelve years and then helped develop microlending programs in Africa, Asia, and Latin America under the auspices of the U.S. Agency for International Development (USAID), Cooperative for American Relief to Everywhere (CARE), Catholic Relief Services, and the United Nations. Having seen various permutations of the strategy, Ashe became interested in designing an approach that could work in the United States. Clearly, the need for the kind of business loans, training, and peer support that these programs provided in the developing world existed here. Ashe decided to try to service that need.

Ashe was teaching at New Hampshire College when he began to work in earnest on the project and got the college-affiliated Institute for Cooperative Community Development (ICCD) to sponsor his concept.[13] He then approached funders for support and launched the project with seed money from the Ford Foundation's Rural Poverty Program.

The initial rural focus of Working Capital was largely circumstantial. The program has become increasingly urban in focus since then. A study conducted for Working Capital by Mt. Auburn Associates found that "while closed (and therefore earlier) loans were 56 percent urban in number and 57 percent in dollar volume, active loans are 77 percent urban in number and 72 percent in dollar volume."[14] Having established a track record, it has become easier for Working Capital to raise funds that have enabled it to expand operations. In addition, the density of urban settings allows for valuable synergistic activity to occur between borrowers and other community organizations.

Metropolitan Boston's *Business Plan for 1995 and Beyond* calls Working Capital "an outstanding organizing tool . . . which develops both leaders and markets." Program staff hope to use the organization of small businesses resulting from participation in Working Capital as a springboard to achieve much more than access to credit. These other goals include creating pressure for change at the local level by speaking out to political and corporate actors and reaching a scale that would enable the loan fund to approach self-sufficiency. With respect to self-sufficiency, Working Capital hopes to reduce its operating costs by charging fees to stable businesses and making larger loans that will help to subsidize smaller ones.

PHILOSOPHY. Ashe modeled Working Capital most closely on Latin America's FINCA, which originally operated by setting up community-

13. Working Capital became an independent nonprofit in September 1993; program headquarters are currently in Cambridge.
14. Mt. Auburn Associates (1994, sec. 4, p. 4).

managed "village banks" that made loans available to groups. The two most important features that Ashe adapted for Working Capital are FINCA's decentralized operation and the high level of responsibility it gives to borrowers. Ashe found these an attractive means of empowerment because they empower borrowers by giving them greater control over the program and they help to keep program costs down. According to Marcy Goldstein-Gelb, who has been with the program since its inception, the philosophy has evolved but has continued to be based on certain underlying principles. One of Ashe's mottoes, "They know how," has served as a constant reminder to program staff that "the borrowers can really make all the decisions." Goldstein-Gelb says that the organization has also built itself using a "piggyback model . . . of tapping into existing resources" such as the business training already offered through other organizations. These two principles help the program maintain the dual focus of decentralization and delegation.

PEER LENDING. Working Capital does all its training and lending in borrowing groups.[15] Group members, with some help from their enterprise agent, meet regularly (usually once a month) to work through the training materials, become chartered, and accept or deny each other's loan applications.

Despite the obvious benefits of the group-lending methodology, Ashe's decision to employ group lending in the Working Capital program ultimately made his initial job as a fund-raiser difficult. Even though many programs in less developed countries had built impressive records using peer lending, funders remained very skeptical about the workability of this method in the United States. Would people actually risk losing money to strangers? Would they invest so much time for such small loans? Ashe remained convinced that group lending could work in the United States and eventually got enough funders on board to start the program.

Working Capital borrowers must begin borrowing at the $500 level and then proceed through successive levels regardless of need, credit history, or size of business. Table 4-1 illustrates the amounts and terms of each step. Borrowers pay interest of approximately 12 percent plus a service fee of between two and five dollars a month to help cover loan administration, business education, and training materials. This process of

---

15. The peer lending concept is discussed in greater detail in chapter 2.

Table 4-1. *Working Capital Stepping Process*

Step	Maximum loan amount ($)	To be paid no faster than (months)
1	500	4–6
2	1,000	4–12
3	1,500	4–18
4	3,000	12–36
5	5,000	12–36

starting out small and progressively borrowing larger sums of money is called "stepping," and is increasingly employed in microenterprise programs, particularly those that use peer lending. During the first couple of rounds, borrowers learn about the process of borrowing and also build trust with each other. Although many participants expressed dissatisfaction with the small size of loans available, they also recognized that borrowing large amounts right away could potentially strain the trust necessary to make the peer group structure work. Marian, who owns and operates a commercial cleaning business with her husband, indicates that she had no reservations about guaranteeing the loans of the other people in her group largely because she "had a good feel for the people." In addition, she said, "when you're talking about $500, going on the hook for that, eh. Even $1,000, eh. Now when you start getting out there, you know, it may be a different thing. But we also have a history now, I think." The theory behind stepping is that by the time group members are ready to borrow sums large enough to potentially damage the credit or business of others, group members know enough about each other's businesses to feel confident about approving, rejecting, or imposing conditions on another member's loan.

The main disadvantage of stepping is that it constrains borrowers whose businesses are growing quickly and who need larger amounts of credit to keep pace with the growth. Manfred, who has moved his rapidly growing graphic design business from his mother's garage to a warehouse space in the year since he joined Working Capital, is experiencing this kind of problem:

The way that their schedule is structured it's just that a company that wants to grow quickly is not going to be able to. . . . It would take me, if I were to rely just solely on Working Capital for this to be an effective company, to make any sort of profit and be in the black, six years . . . I think that the lending should coincide with growth. That's like if you can pay back $500 in a week, do it, and you've still got that on your credit rating as paying it off.

Manfred has begun to look for other sources of capital, but they are few and far between. Herb chooses not to focus on the small size of the loans but rather on the fact that Working Capital is providing any access to capital at all. To Herb, the glass is half full. When potential participants grumble about the small loans, Herb tells them, "You might complain, but there's no other game in town."

Manfred's situation illustrates the problem with stepping. On the one hand, it works well with the group-lending process because it lessens the risk that group members assume. If the primary goal of the program is to empower communities and build a strong network of small businesses, the program may be fine as it is. It accomplishes these goals effectively. On the other hand, if a goal of the program is to motivate economic development in disadvantaged communities, these small loans will not go very far in that direction unless the program is taking a very long-term view and a "next lender" exists to serve businesses that have outgrown the capacity of Working Capital.

Ashe and others at Working Capital recognize that the demand for larger loans exists and that meeting this demand would serve program goals of fostering economic development and creating a more cost-effective program: larger loans cost less to administer per dollar lent and bring in more in interest income to the program, thereby subsidizing both smaller loans and operating costs. The disadvantage of making larger loans is that they expose the program and individual borrowers to greater risk. "What we don't want to do is have one business go down the tubes and everybody else gets pulled down with it," Wilson asserts. Stepping works in part because the risk is relatively low. Also, the fact that borrowers cannot progress too rapidly from one level to the next gives members an opportunity to establish some history together. As Wilson states, "It takes time before people really know who's bankable or not within the group."

Working Capital staff recognize, however, that there is a market of entrepreneurs who need larger loans, who are not currently being served, and some of whom are program participants. Because the Metro Boston project had been in existence for less than two years when this research was conducted, pressure for larger amounts of money was not too intense; most borrowers were still at the $1,000 level. Still, Working Capital would like to serve this market and is currently grappling with how best to do so. The most likely development would consist of making larger loans as an extension of what the program already does. Borrowers would still have to proceed through the same levels at the predetermined pace, but the ceiling would be raised to $10,000 or more. Program staff are also interested in serving a tier of borrowers who would come in at the $5,000 or $10,000 level, but all agree that this kind of project would have to proceed very cautiously and carefully test the changes on a pilot group.

WORKING CAPITAL AND THE ECONOMIC DEVELOPMENT–SOCIAL WELFARE CONTINUUM. Like Women's Initiative, Working Capital combats the problem of persistent urban poverty in a somewhat indirect way. Arguably the most important thing the program accomplishes with respect to poverty is to create and strengthen networks in poor, urban communities. These networks, which are discussed in greater detail in chapter 6, are an important step in community development. Most participants reported that, while they may be running their businesses smarter and more efficiently, the size of their businesses and the income they generate have not expanded much. The value added from participating in the program comes from belonging to a network that provides support, information, and a sense of community. The extent to which these networks translate into the alleviation of urban poverty remains to be seen; because the program emphasizes building social capital rather than financial capital, its effects will only be realized in the long term.

One of the limitations of Working Capital lies in the lending methodology of the program. The very small first loan coupled with the steps through which all participants must proceed means that unless borrowers can get access to other sources of capital, their businesses will not grow very quickly. Only after several generations of borrowers have succeeded in reaching the larger loan levels will there be the potential for visible change at the community level. The problem of lack of training also inhibits participants from running their businesses more effectively and building them up more quickly. For the least advantaged participants, the training may not be basic enough and may require them to be motivated to an extent that is unrealistic. This group may require greater structure than Working Capital can offer. The program clearly works best for borrowers who bring some experience and some basic business know-how to the table. At the same time, the community-oriented focus on network formation may lay the foundation for poverty alleviation in the longer term.

The staff of Working Capital largely agree that by itself the program cannot have a significant economic development impact in the Boston neighborhoods it targets. At the same time, they are quick to point out that by creating a network of two hundred businesses and providing them with credit and training in less than two years, they have done more than most agencies. Goldstein-Gelb believes that Working Capital is a vehicle within the realm of community economic development strategies that, by definition, help to alleviate poverty.

Inasmuch as Working Capital targets people who are clear about their desire to be self-employed and makes these businesses more productive by providing them with capital and training, there is an economic development outcome, albeit small. The Mt. Auburn study found that Working Capital has had "a very positive impact on business formation and expansion. The vast majority of businesses operated by program participants have survived and become stronger."[16] This same study found that although the average amount of income taken out of the business every month had increased by about 18 percent as a result of program participation, personal income derived from the businesses remained fairly small and probably insufficient to fully support participants.

As for the individual empowerment that is so much a part of what Women's Initiative does, Working Capital staff recognize that confidence building and empowerment happen as a result of participating in the program but claim that it is more of "an unintentional by-product" than an explicit goal. Their primary concern is "creating the conditions of commerce," which they hope to achieve by building a web of small businesses operating throughout disenfranchised communities. The goals of Working Capital and the method with which it has attempted to achieve them place it closer to the economic development side of the continuum than to the social welfare side. In terms of its impacts and outcomes, however, it is probably closer to the middle.

Complications of Life in the Middle

Their operational differences aside, the programs discussed in this chapter have clearly had similar experiences. They all blend aspects of economic

16. Mt. Auburn Associates (1994, sec. 4, p. 31).

development and poverty alleviation strategies. The results are overwhelmingly beneficial; the programs work in places and with people that traditional programs largely fail to reach. They serve a niche in the population that is a poor fit with workfare programs. Often these people cannot find suitable work elsewhere, other responsibilities necessitate that they generate income from their homes, and they are attached to the place they live even though job opportunities are few. This section documents the complexity of working in the interstices of two separate spheres.

Programs Have Difficulty Toeing the Evaluation Line

As mentioned earlier, it is difficult to evaluate microenterprise programs precisely because they integrate aspects of economic development and poverty alleviation strategies. Indicators used to evaluate economic development programs are generally quantitative and include changes in jobs created, income, and the number of businesses in a given area. Indicators used to evaluate poverty alleviation strategies or social welfare programs often consist of more qualitative categories such as changes in self-esteem and family stability.

Not only do microenterprise programs incorporate both kinds of goals, but the weight accorded one function or the other (which is often manifested by the resources it devotes to training and lending) differs greatly from one program to the next. Delma Soto, executive director of Accion New York, explains that in her program

> every decision that's made is based on a business implication as opposed to a social [one]. . . . The social aspect happens as a result of making the right business decisions. . . . We're providing people with an opportunity to grow their business. And by growing their business and earning more income, there's a whole list of things that result from that. Empowerment is just one of them.

This stance results partly from the fact that Accion works only with businesses that have been established for at least one year. Women's Initiative works with any woman who meets the income criteria and wants to explore self-employment. According to Miriam Walden, this means that

> Women's Initiative has chosen to work with a group of people who, in general, require assistance in preparing their ability to argue for a loan and their ability to repay it. So that means you have to take on

the training challenge in order to do it. And then training is a big and expensive thing . . . so naturally it looks like the organization is mostly training. . . . And the other side of the question is that I think it's always been an expressed belief of this organization that . . . training is actually more important than lending, and that our primary mission is to do training and not lending.

To some extent, the philosophies of Accion and Women's Initiative represent opposites. The position that each holds is dynamic rather than static, however. Accion is exploring ways to incorporate more training into its program, and Women's Initiative has begun to generate additional loan products.

The larger point of these stories is that the wide variety of positions programs take makes it extremely difficult for funders—public or private—to evaluate and compare programs. The quotations above suggest that Accion behaves like an economic development program in which the goal is to create jobs and raise income. Women's Initiative operates more along the lines of a training program, in which development of skills must occur before employment goals are reached. Although both programs exist under the microenterprise umbrella, the different orientation of each requires a different yardstick that grows out of a deep understanding of program philosophies and goals.

Microenterprise Strategy Is Neither People-Based nor Place-Based

The debate over whether strategies should focus on people or on places reinforces the split between economic development and social welfare. Economic development strategies generally target places; social welfare programs tend to focus on people. Strategies that target people often categorize them according to attributes such as socioeconomic class and education or skill level. These strategies also look at broader characteristics that are correlated with weak attachment to the labor force, such as gender and race, as well as various other factors that have left the client at a disadvantage.

Microenterprise programs focus on individuals yet are deeply rooted in the context of the places in which they operate. This inherent dualism helps them avoid many of the typical problems of place-based and people-oriented strategies. The programs do not restrict economic and residential mobility, as some place-based programs do, nor do they attempt to reform so-called aberrant behaviors. Future policy efforts directed at the persistently poor should strive to achieve a similar balance, which must begin with helping the individual and understanding that person as a product and member of a geographic community.

Conclusion

The processes and outcomes of the three programs examined in this chapter demonstrate the variety of ways in which the microenterprise strategy blurs the line between economic development and social welfare. Although microenterprise programs will not remove poverty, neither will any other single program. Microenterprise programs do provide a motivated population with services it does not receive elsewhere. And although the programs do not exhibit outstanding numbers in terms of traditional economic development indicators—jobs created, income generated, and so on—they have the potential to produce strong second- and third-order outcomes. These include the formation of social and human capital, the spread of economic literacy, and the transformation of disenfranchised people into economic actors. Blurring the boundaries allows investment in social capital to help people become self-sufficient in the long run rather than maintain them in the short run. And the benefits of investment, by definition, take some time to accrue.

FIVE

Self-Employment and the Welfare Problem

THE RECENT LEGISLATION moving recipients from welfare to work has produced increasing interest in the potential of self-employment, particularly for low-income women who are heads of households. Can microenterprise programs be used as a strategy to help them become economically self-sufficient? Many low-income household heads pursue self-employment as a way to make ends meet. However, this group, particularly the poor women who make up most of it, often lacks access to credit, training, and other important self-employment resources, precisely those that microenterprise programs provide.[1] Although microenterprise programs intuitively make sense as a way to help the group solve its problems, income from self-employment, it must be remembered, rarely supports the family by itself. Rather, it contributes to the family's income package.[2]

This chapter examines that contribution and gauges whether and how it can be expanded to help this group more closely approach self-sufficiency. Although microenterprise programs clearly can be critical in fostering and stabilizing the self-employment activity of low-income people, self-employment is likely to be neither a certain nor an easy route off welfare. The situation is discussed from the perspective of Women's Initiative (San Francisco–Oakland), ISED (Iowa), and WHEDCO (South Bronx). These programs were selected because of their geographic placement (they

1. Spalter-Roth, Soto, and Zandniapour (1994).
2. Spalter-Roth and others (1994); Servon (1996, 1997); Servon and Bates (1998).

represent three different policy environments and demographically different settings) and their commitment to serving people with very low income. Many microenterprise programs, recognizing the high cost and amount of training this population tends to require, have decided to target a higher socioeconomic group, which is generally cheaper and easier to serve.[3]

The interviews exposed many welfare-reliant entrepreneurs and potential entrepreneurs who are current or former public assistance recipients. Those who are able to use self-employment to leave welfare tend to have several characteristics in common: solid support networks, some experience in their line of business, and a strong desire to get off welfare. Interviews with program staff and nonparticipant observation at programs disclosed the kinds of services and support that these people require. In most cases income generated from self-employment has been a necessary but not sufficient ingredient for those who have made the transition from welfare.

The Attraction of Self-Employment

Program participants varied widely in the reasons they gave for turning to public assistance and for pursuing self-employment. The interest in self-employment, however, seemed most prevalent among two categories of people: true entrepreneurs who would always prefer to work for themselves even if this does not appear to be an economically rational decision (they may work for lower wages and for longer hours in self-employment than they would by getting a job); and those for whom self-employment is the best available option.

True Entrepreneurs

True entrepreneurs pursue self-employment because they do not seem to fit into the mainstream economy. Several I interviewed had had training in various skills but were unable to settle into a regular job. As men-

3. The clients interviewed were diverse in their program experience, business type, and demographic characteristics. The core of the research for this chapter consisted of thirty in-depth interviews conducted with current and former public assistance recipients who are considering or using self-employment as a route off welfare. Twenty-six interviews were conducted with single mothers; two with single fathers; two with married couples with children who are jointly operating their businesses; and two with women who were single mothers when they received public assistance but are now married to men who are the primary earners in their households.

tioned in chapter 3, Grace had worked as a nurse's aide and had obtained her cosmetology license before she went into the daycare business. Her present income comes from a combination of doing hair for a couple of regular clients, public assistance, and from her business. In the case of Dwight, Sangeetha, and Dan, conflicts with their former employers proved a strong motivating factor. At the same time, Dan liked "calling your own shots," and not feeling the "shackles." Another common reason for self-employment among the entrepreneurs was that they believed in their product and got a great deal of satisfaction out of making customers happy.

Best Available Option

This category can be divided into several groups: people who would gladly work for wages if they could make enough to support their families; people whose life paths were interrupted by an unplanned pregnancy, a job layoff, the dissolution of a marriage, and so on. Three of the entrepreneurs interviewed in Iowa began receiving public assistance after losing well-paid factory jobs. They did not consider low-wage work without benefits to be an option, largely because it did not pay enough to allow them to afford child care and did not provide medical benefits for their children. Self-employment offered more hope and opportunity than other low-wage, unstable jobs. Angie, a single mother of three without child support, opted for this solution when she lost her $10-an-hour job with a meat-packing company because it was closing. She was in the middle of buying a house at the time and felt that "without a college degree I couldn't get a job that would support us, so it was kind of sink or swim." Her struggle, as explained in chapter 3, has required a great deal of sacrifice. In retrospect, if she had had the choice, she would not necessarily have gone into business because of the dedication it takes. But, she said, it was really her only option.

The case of Jim, also described in chapter 3, typifies the move to welfare because of a difficult family situation. Abandoned by his wife, Jim had to leave a paying job to look after his two daughters. He went on public assistance and began a television repair business in his basement, which he gradually expanded with the help of ISED, family support, and Iowa's waiver program. The location is close to home and allows him to get away if one of the girls is sick.

Like the true entrepreneurs, many of those who originally pursued self-employment because of an unplanned event claim that they much prefer self-employment to working for someone else. The advantages they cite include flexibility, control, pride in what they do, and freedom. The disadvantages include long hours, unreliable income, and lack of benefits.

Barriers to the Pursuit of Self-Employment

Although self-employment fits the life situations of welfare-reliant, potential entrepreneurs in many respects, their transition to self-employment is a rocky road. The challenges of single parenthood and a lack of necessary support—financial and emotional—can make self-employment a distant dream for some until they can stabilize other parts of their lives. Several people I interviewed have gone through the training provided by the programs but are not yet in business. Tanya would like to become a desktop publisher and has been through the Women's Initiative business planning class twice. She recently had her third child, however, and had to move back in with her aunt. Her self-employment plans are "on the back burner for now." Asked what she needs to have in place before she can become self-employed, Tanya answered,

> It's really like a puzzle, and if one piece falls off, like the child care, or your money is cut, you cannot do it. I really want to get off, but if I went to work, I could not get my energy together to do my business. I do not want to get off until I have my business, but that stops me, too, because I do not have enough money to do anything, so it's a Catch-22.

Some of these participants either drop out of the courses before finishing or they finish without starting businesses, only to return once they have eliminated some of the barriers that blocked them earlier. They may decide that they need more training, that they must wait until their children are old enough to go to school, or that they need to move out of an unstable or unhealthy home environment before they can take on the commitment that self-employment entails. In most evaluations these people are classified as dropouts, and those who return to programs or pursue other strategies are not tracked.

However, interviews revealed that it was not uncommon for dropouts to return to both ISED and Women's Initiative (WHEDCO is still too new for this to happen). Lorraine went to ISED the first time with the intention of starting a hog farm but did not finish because "I decided my business idea wasn't any good. . . . It was too expensive." The second time, when she went with the idea of doing business services, she was much better prepared and sailed through the three remaining classes. Elaine went through the program three times before putting together the will and the business idea that allowed her to succeed. After spending several years on welfare, she started her cleaning business in June 1996 and left public assistance in February 1997. She now has three full-time employees and has begun to diversify, expanding into new cleaning niches and buying real estate. When asked what the difference was between coming to ISED the first time and finally being able to launch her business, Elaine said, "It wasn't the right time. You know I've thought a lot about that and I think that in my mind I was just ready this time. They do a lot with self-esteem and I think that at first I thought, 'Oh, that's not me they're talking about.' And now I can see that that was exactly what was going on. Self-esteem was a big issue for me." Mel Essex, an ISED trainer in the Waterloo office, reports that there have been four or five business starts from previous clients in the last few months. "I think they come back because we cared about them the first time," says Mel.

Experiences with the Welfare System

None of those interviewed described their experiences with the welfare system in a positive way. Two eventually found caseworkers who helped them pursue self-employment. The difficulties with the welfare system fell into five categories: constantly battling the welfare system bureaucracy, inappropriate programs, the lack of recognition for efforts to leave through self-employment or education, distinctions between themselves and other recipients, and fears about child care and health care.

Bureaucracy

Participants' experiences with the welfare system varied depending in part on where they lived. Iowans generally had fewer gripes, presumably because of that state's relatively generous waiver system. Those living in California and New York complained of battling the bureaucracy while trying to make their businesses viable. Maintaining eligibility for benefits is a constant difficulty in all three states. Even in Iowa's program, participants who have committed themselves to the pursuit of self-employment must report their hourly activities to caseworkers to prove that they are devoting themselves to their business full time.

Sangeetha and Dan participate in an experimental California program called Families for Self-Sufficiency that provides them with a housing subsidy and allows them to run their business producing and selling chutney and curry powders. Although their business has grown tremendously in the past three years, they continue to struggle every month, and their income fluctuates a great deal. When either one of them takes on extra work to save some money or generate cash for business supplies, their benefits are immediately cut. Four years after starting the business, Sangeetha says,

> Yes, we still come to the point of "what's going to be for dinner." Still. That's what really makes me sad about the social service system. . . . Once I got a letter from the social service woman that just blew my head. She canceled my food stamps because I had $120 savings in the bank which I could use for food. That was four years worth of savings for my kid! If he got sick, I would take the money, but not for us to eat.

Even in Iowa, participants had difficulty dealing with the bureaucracy. Jim claims that, although he was on a waiver,

> they cut my benefits so low the only thing I could pay was gas and lights. I went around and around with DHS [Department of Human Services]. It took a good six or seven months to get it straightened out and I couldn't pay rent on my store that whole time so I was lucky I had such a good landlord. . . . I picked up a second job for awhile at night in a bar. I worked under the table just to make some extra money.

Recognizing the dual nature of Iowa's system, Kristy, who had just graduated from ISED when I interviewed her, said, "I look at welfare as help, and then a ball and chain sometimes." Marge, who runs a children's consignment store in a rural Iowa community, went on public assistance briefly during a period in which she was separated from her husband. She claimed that she was repeatedly "interrogated" because "they didn't believe I was living on just [my welfare check]. They don't act like you're a human being half the time."

Inappropriate Programs

Interviewees at all three programs complained the welfare system offered them jobs that did not match their skill level and goals. Most were willing to work to leave welfare, but not in demeaning jobs that would not pay a living wage. Samantha, who has been on welfare for twelve years, wanted to go to school but was required to participate in California's GAIN program instead.

> They let me sit home all day and collect money, but when I wanted to go take classes, "No, no," they said. They made me go to this GAIN program. I didn't learn anything there. They tell you to look in the phone book and pick out seven jobs and go for them . . . at places like McDonald's! I told them this about McDonald's: I'm not that smart but I took a calculator, and I know I would be worse off than being on welfare if I worked there because I would not get any benefits. What if something happened to my kid? When I was in that program, I cried every night. It's a training program, but they don't assess who you are. They make everybody do the same retarded work, although the lady next to me had a master's degree, and the one on the other side was still on drugs. It's out of control.

Similarly, Tamika decided to put all of her energy into her home-based daycare business after she refused to accept a low-level cleaning job through New York's Work Experience Program (WEP), the state's response to welfare reform. Her benefits were cut immediately. Luckily, she took on two new children that same week, which allowed her to survive, although neither she nor her daughter currently has any health insurance. Tamika says that if the jobs WEP offered would have put her on the path to a career, she would have been happy to have taken one. Instead, she is going to school part-time and working to make her business viable enough to support her and her daughter until she gets her degree. Kristy feels that "there are people there who still need help with going back to get their GED. I'm mixed in right with those people, you know, different standings. . . . Get me out of there, put me somewhere else. There needs to be separate programs."

These stories describe a system that is so large and unwieldy that it cannot match the unique package of needs, skills, limits, and strengths of each recipient with an appropriate route out. Iowa comes closest. Every welfare recipient, along with a caseworker, constructs a family investment agreement detailing what they will do to begin to remove obstacles to attaining self-sufficiency. The state provides resources, such as tuition assistance and child care, to participants that need them to realize their plan. Following the passage of the Personal Responsibility and Work Opportunity Reconciliation Act of 1996, other states have begun to experiment with similar systems. No state system has mastered the art of delivering the kind of attention many recipients need, however. According to Marge, the primary problem is that "the system is so big and they need to know that these are people, individuals. . . . They can't use the same guidelines and rules for everyone."

Distinction between Themselves and Other Recipients

Most of the welfare recipients interviewed saw themselves as different from the majority of welfare recipients they encountered at social service agencies, in training programs, and in their neighborhoods. Many believe that welfare fraud is widespread and that they are punished for their own honesty because of those who cheat the system. According to Sangeetha,

> I don't hide a penny from them, and if Dan does a part-time job, when I do one, we always report it. . . . Meanwhile, I see women coming into the welfare office with jewelry and kids that are beautifully dressed. And me, sometimes I couldn't get a new pair of shoes. One day I cried because I saw a woman get her check and hop into a brand new car, and there I was waiting for the bus. For me, working as hard as I do, and I have to come in for three, four hours every month.

In a similar vein, Kristy complains that "there are many, many, too many people on welfare just to be on welfare. They aren't going anywhere, baby after baby. You know, the typical thing, what everybody thinks. And that's why when people hear that I'm on welfare, it's always the stereotype. There are people out there like me who do need the help." Tanya believes that welfare reform "is scary, but it is also good because a lot of people do not need to be on it, they need to do something. It made a lot of men and women lazy." This tendency to draw distinctions between themselves and other welfare recipients probably helps to motivate this group to get off welfare. At the same time, it also works to fragment a group that shares common interests and could be working together to build a coalition and argue for meaningful change.

Lack of Recognition for Attempts to Leave Welfare

Nearly all of the interviewees believed that the welfare system failed to recognize their good faith efforts to work themselves off public assistance and save for their children. Although a few of those interviewed had found a caseworker who was sympathetic to their efforts, most felt that they were continually battling to maintain what they needed to survive and that the expenditure of this effort both took away from their businesses and left them feeling depressed. Randy says:

> Over there at the welfare office they call me Mr. Appeal Man because I appeal everything they send to the house. I'd do monthly reports and what I made gross, they'd cut my check. But they weren't looking at what's my bills down here [at the store]. Until you live like this, you don't understand. They can go home every night and do whatever they want, go shopping. Right now, I'm battling Christmas. You can work hard but you need a break.

In general, entrepreneurs believed that the people they worked with in the social welfare system did not trust them to correctly report earnings from the business. Many reported having their benefits erroneously cut swiftly and working for months to get the system corrected while their businesses and households suffered because of the unexpected drop in funds. Most small businesses are vulnerable enough that this kind of sudden change in income can destroy their fragile equilibrium. According to Sangeetha and Dan's logic, "The system saves money if people get themselves better and get off in the long run, so why do you look at someone like that as taking advantage?"

Child Care and Health Care

Few public assistance recipients were worried about the time limits they will face under welfare reform. Many expressed greater concern about women who lacked resources, skills, and motivation. Those interviewed considered themselves relatively advantaged but in need of some help to become self-sufficient. Most claimed that they could find a job if they were forced to work, but that they had not been able to find jobs that would pay them a living wage and allow them to take care of their children. Some stated that they would work now if they had access to child care, while others maintained that it was most important for them to raise their young children themselves. Lily, who has an infant daughter and schools her thirteen-year-old at home, explained,

> When I had just one child, I worked and that was fine. But after I had the second daughter and the father bailed, I researched child

care and found there was no way I could afford it. That's when I went on the system. . . . What they [policymakers] don't see is that raising your children *is* doing something. It is not valued in our society, but it is something.

Tanya, considering the trade-offs between welfare and work, claimed, "I can get a job, that is not the problem. It's the child care! Child care would take that check, so why even go to work. It starts to bother me after a while, but I have to be picky. I need a $10 [an hour] job to pay for child care and transportation."

Every person interviewed expressed the most concern about access to health care. Several who have left AFDC/TANF are being careful to maintain eligibility for medicaid for as long as possible. Most saw public assistance as the only way to obtain some income and medical insurance while caring for their children. All these parents were most worried about how they would get access to medical care once they were forced off welfare. When asked how she felt about welfare reform, Grace, the Iowan who runs a daycare business, answered, "It doesn't bother me. I don't get much, and if I have to get a part-time job, I will. My only concern is about medical coverage. There are four asthmatics in my house, and we really need that coverage." In a similar vein, when asked what she would tell policymakers about how to improve the welfare system if she had the opportunity, Angie stated, "There needs to be an insurance program that goes along with this [welfare reform]. You can cut back on other things, but when you have to take your kid to the doctor to get medicine, you just have to do it. And then you're paying for months and months."

For these parents, self-employment is attractive precisely because it offers them the flexibility to care for their children while generating some income. However, single parents, who need flexibility most, also need reliable income, and the demands of single parenthood clearly make it very difficult for people like Lily and Tanya, both of whom have infant children and have been unable to launch their businesses, to devote the time and energy necessary to develop businesses capable of supporting a family. For those who do have businesses, their lack of health insurance makes the businesses even more vulnerable. One prolonged illness or a single accident could take them away from a business that is highly dependent on them or leave them with medical bills that they cannot pay and therefore spoil their credit rating.

Characteristics of Successful Entrepreneurs

Interviews with current and prospective entrepreneurs suggest that welfare recipients who are able to use self-employment as an exit strategy are a small population within the larger universe of people who rely on welfare. What characteristics do entrepreneurs who have been able to leave welfare share? Anecdotal evidence suggests that the experience of participating in a microenterprise program helps people succeed in other ways as well, such as giving them the skills and self-confidence they need to obtain a job in the mainstream economy. I define success more narrowly and include only self-employment because the goal here is to determine the feasibility of this strategy for welfare recipients. The three characteristics that all successful entrepreneurs studied hold in common are their ability to tap into strong support networks, experience or training in their line of business, and fierce determination.

Strong and Reliable Support Networks

Entrepreneurs who have successfully made the transition from welfare to self-employment have a solid support network of family and friends to help them fulfill the household and economic obligations that single parents must meet simultaneously. Angie's mother and Jim's brother watch their stores when they need to be elsewhere, and Grace's sister helps her with financial planning and bookkeeping. Dwight's parents and Jim's father watch their children after school. Home-based daycare providers in New York City are required to have a backup person who has been screened and can watch the children in an emergency. Vivian's sister is her backup person, and Tamika has a friend who helps her. In exchange, Tamika watches her friend's children while their mother goes to school. Others had help from family and friends with renovations to their storefronts and donations of other necessities.

Microenterprise programs clearly add to and strengthen these networks. Many of the entrepreneurs interviewed spoke of the importance of the relationships they had forged with the business consultants and trainers at microenterprise programs. These relationships, which are discussed in chapter 6, boost self-confidence and get entrepreneurs to a place that enables them seriously to pursue their businesses. Most of the successful entrepreneurs maintain these relationships after graduation and continue to use them as a resource to obtain access to information, funding, and other resources.

Prior Experience or Training in Their Business

Having the skills required to produce their product or service gives these entrepreneurs a head start and allows them to focus on the business aspect of entrepreneurship. Jim learned how to repair televisions from his parents. Grace's mother is a daycare provider. Dwight honed his skills repairing small engines for his previous employer before opening his own shop. In some cases the entrepreneurs interviewed had worked for someone else in their business and decided to start their own business because they believed they did better work or because they did not like the idea of doing the work without making the profit. Cindy started her cleaning business after working for someone else. "She would pay me six bucks an hour and I would see her pick these checks up for $60 and I would think, "I just cleaned this house and she got $60 and I got $15." I thought, something's not right. I can do this myself." Entrepreneurs with an existing skill already know how to produce their good or service. Many also know where to obtain supplies and how to market and price their product.

Determination and Resourcefulness

Many of the entrepreneurs defined success for themselves as getting off welfare. Many felt ashamed for having to rely on public assistance. Others described their experiences with the welfare system as depressing and so tedious that they wanted to have nothing to do with the bureaucracy. Most wanted to be good role models for their children and wanted to work for their own money. The desire to leave welfare often drove their determination.

Examples of entrepreneurs' resourcefulness and ability to start a business on a shoestring abound. Dwight could not afford to buy much of the equipment he needed for his machine shop, so he improvised by building his own using cast-off equipment that he salvaged. He was able to get a bank loan for $15,000 that he stretched by buying machinery he could not make and plumbing supplies for the system he installed himself. His workshop, in a shed next to his house, is heated only with a woodburning stove. Successful entrepreneurs work very long hours and invest enormous amounts of energy into their businesses. Sangeetha recalled that "in the first few years, when [our son] was very little, it was very hard. I was working until late at night, coming home with blisters on my hands. We have just put so much energy in this business. Sometimes I thought I could not do this any more. But the next day you go again." The entrepreneurs interviewed work well in excess of a standard forty-hour week—most work 60–80 hours. And when times get tough they work harder, either putting more energy into their businesses or picking up extra sidework to bridge the rough spot.

Lessons from Programs

The term *microenterprise program* covers a variety of programs with different missions, methods, and target populations. All three of the programs studied for this chapter are similar in that they have maintained a commitment to serving entrepreneurs with a very low income. This commitment means that they resemble each other. First, the range of services offered and the amount of time spent training and supporting clients are both broad and deep. Second, the relationships forged between entrepreneurs, program staff, and other participants are strong and important to participants' success. The relationships often serve the purposes that are filled by family, friends, and other work- or education-related networks in more advantaged populations. Serving welfare recipients means that these programs must provide services beyond credit. Most microenterprise programs do not target people with a very low income to the extent that the three programs studied here do.

The programs experience a range of challenges. For Women's Initiative, the two biggest challenges have been how to appropriately assess women for entrepreneurial readiness and how to best serve women currently dependent on public assistance. Other research suggests that difficulty serving poor people is a common problem among microenterprise programs.[4] ISED's collaboration with Iowa's Department of Human Services and its initial mission to serve welfare recipients have enabled it to reach the welfare-reliant population more effectively than most.

Business consultants at all three programs have struggled with getting entrepreneurs to see their self-employment activity as a real business. Although many relied on income from self-employment before participating in microenterprise programs, they did not take themselves seriously until

4. Servon (1998a).

they learned business basics. According to some of the trainers, the ability to view their income-generating activity as business activity required a boost in self-esteem and self-confidence, which is a goal of the training in all three programs.

Because no program serves people on a very low income exclusively, staff at all three discussed the difficulties of serving a population with varied skill levels and needs. All three programs also serve people who are in the planning stages of their business as well as those who are already in business. Some need help with basic literacy skills while others are more advanced and need more concrete information and direction. Some programs discuss offering different classes for people at different levels, but doing so would stretch program resources. In addition, most staff believe that there is value in keeping the classroom diverse and creating an environment in which different kinds of people can learn from one another and in which welfare recipients are not stigmatized.

All programs do some screening to discourage potential entrepreneurs who are not ready to move ahead with self-employment. Program staffs also know they cannot afford to waste scarce resources. At the same time, they do not want to discourage people who are trying to move their lives in a new direction. All three programs review applications of potential participants before they begin training. Women's Initiative recently initiated a formal, multistep screening and assessment. All three help participants determine for themselves whether they are ready, rather than choosing not to accept them. Participants in the ISED program are only "enrolled" in the program after they have attended the first four classes, at which point they must make a conscious decision to move forward and seriously pursue their business. The first two to three weeks of the class deal extensively with self-esteem issues and help potential entrepreneurs decide whether they are ready to be in business. According to Joan Hills, assistant director at ISED,

> All the time, we're talking about the time commitment that you need. The third week, all of this is reviewed again, and we talk about it, and look at that feasibility of their business, and talk about commitment. It seems better to make this the point at which people decide whether to stick with it. As a result, people are more committed to the business, if they go ahead with the business.

Women's Initiative clients attend a two-week business and personal assessment course that fills much the same purposes as the first four weeks at ISED and then choose whether to go on, at which point they must apply for the fourteen-week business development course. Maria-Elena, who runs the food sector training at WHEDCO, asks people who are not sure about pursuing self-employment to sit in on a course as observers before actually enrolling. For the most part, these screening processes consist of well-defined sessions between program staff and participants. Screening, in whatever form it takes, is designed to give participants who may not have a realistic understanding of what it means to start a business a real sense of what is involved.

Success does not always mean starting a business. Programs have found that during training, participants often realize that they are not ready to start businesses or that self-employment is not their best option. The training, however, provides them with skills that are transferable. Those who do not choose to pursue self-employment obtain the skills and self-confidence to use other routes such as mainstream employment to achieve self-sufficiency. Writing a business plan, which two of the three programs require, calls for research skills, writing skills, and the ability to work with numbers to forecast costs and sales.[5] Programs also work with participants to present their ideas out loud and on paper, clearly and convincingly. If nothing else, the experience of going through microenterprise training appears to give welfare recipients a critical jump-start. Asked what she would be doing if she had not gone to ISED, Kristy replied, "I'd be sitting at home. . . . It changed my whole state of mind, my mental and physical attitude. It makes you get up, get the kid off to school, go to the library, and do the research for the business. . . . It was kind of like therapy." Those who do not pursue self-employment often look for a regular job, and these skills can make the difference between success and failure on the job market. Jack Litzenberg, poverty team coordinator of the Charles Stewart Mott Foundation and a longtime supporter of the microenterprise strategy, calls microenterprise programs "the best community education programs in the country."

In fact, staff at all three programs also believe that those who do go through training but do not start businesses bring valuable skills with them to the workplace. Both ISED and WHEDCO are working on ways to formalize these links to this group of clients and the mainstream economy. ISED is considering how to help clients who have been through the pro-

5. Women's Initiative requires a business plan for larger loan requests and offers an optional course designed to guide clients through writing their business plans.

gram but are not ready to become entrepreneurs to use the skills they have learned. Jason Friedman has begun to conceptualize a network made up of employers who would be willing to interview those who have completed ISED's training. ISED would effectively provide a screen for these employers. Women's Initiative connects clients with a job placement and retention program that focuses on jobs in small business. WHEDCO already runs complementary programs, particularly in food service. The program trains people to work in the industry, runs its own catering company, and develops a line of food products for retail sale. WHEDCO will be able to funnel clients who go through microenterprise training for the food industry into one of these programs or into a job using its contacts.

Whether or not clients start businesses, many interviewees were attracted to self-employment training because, unlike traditional welfare-to-work programs, microenterprise programs prepare people for work that offers them hope. New York's WEP participants work cleaning parks and doing maintenance in housing projects, jobs that pay little and are not challenging. Microenterprise programs train them to think critically, prepare for jobs they want to do, and help them think about themselves and their careers in a long-term way.

Self-Employment Income and Low-Income Households

Self-employment is a survival strategy for many but a secure one for few. Although many of the entrepreneurs interviewed for this research have used self-employment successfully to leave welfare entirely, the self-employment income they generate remains low and is often unpredictable. Sangeetha and Dan have housing assistance as well as food stamps and medicaid. Asked whether the business supports them otherwise at this stage, Dan replied,

> We take an average of $550 a month out of the business. That's two people fifty to sixty hours a week. The business income is consistent now, but of course that does not meet our requirements. So Sangeetha caters on the outside, she does child care, I deliver, I do landscaping. It's all self-employment.

WHEDCO's home-based daycare providers enjoy running their own businesses because self-employment allows them to do things their way and affords them the flexibility to care for their own children and do other things. For example, two of the women interviewed were attending community college. However, all complained about the inherent instability of their business income. As Tamika describes it, "I may have a child for six months and then the parent decides not to send them and I'm counting on that money. It's always up and down like that, so you can't really depend on it."

Most of the entrepreneurs interviewed were income packagers on welfare and continue to package self-employment income with income from other sources. Several of the ISED entrepreneurs do farm work for extra money during heavy seasons. In addition to her welfare check, Lily, a Women's Initiative client who has not yet started a business, receives income that she does not report from one of her children's fathers and also earns extra money driving for an elderly woman. Vivian does not report all of the child care money she brings in; reporting too much would cause her to lose her food stamps and medicaid benefits, which she needs to get by. Lorraine has relied on public assistance for most of the thirteen years since her son was born. She discovered she was pregnant while undergoing the physical exams required for entry into the air force. In 1991 she started a business doing bookkeeping for grain farmers and providing other business services from her home. During the past year, when she was still on a waiver, she supplemented her public assistance and business income with $800 from selling vegetables from her garden, $800 helping her parents on their farm, and $500 from painting and wallpapering.

These families continue to struggle and to think of innovative ways to make enough money to make ends meet. This finding supports other research that shows that neither low-wage work nor welfare on its own is sufficient for families to live.[6] Self-employment earnings are one important source of income and help stabilize family incomes.

Conclusion

Obtaining a stable income from self-employment can take many years; potential entrepreneurs need a safety net while starting. Public assistance programs must recognize good-faith efforts of recipients to get off welfare. Several entrepreneurs told stories of being unable to save for education or to start their business. Others, particularly those in New York, were unable to complete self-employment training because they were forced to participate in workfare programs, which can get in the way of efforts

6. Edin and Lein (1997).

that increase recipients' personal assets (education, self-employment) but take a long time to bear fruit. States should therefore allow welfare-reliant entrepreneurs to continue to receive benefits while they start their businesses. Staffs at all three programs recognize the difficulty of achieving independence through self-employment, and expressed concern that funders and policymakers seemed to believe that participants could become self-sufficient in less than a year. Over and over, the staffs emphasized that the move toward self-sufficiency includes both progress and setbacks. States therefore need to provide transitional benefits for those who pursue self-employment as a way of leaving welfare. The Iowa waiver program, which allows welfare recipients to continue to collect benefits while stabilizing their businesses, can perhaps provide a template for other states to follow.

Self-employment must be supported as an option for the segment of the welfare population that is prepared to pursue it. Although the participants who have been able to make the transition from welfare to self-employment are not representative of the larger welfare population, the support they have received through microenterprise programs has been critical to their success. Staffs at all three programs agree that self-employment will only work for a small percentage of the welfare-reliant population, but it is important to find solutions that work for different groups rather than continue to search for a silver bullet. Support for a variety of solutions makes sense, given the range of reasons why people become dependent on welfare in the first place. Self-employment has allowed those interviewed for this study to support their families financially and to be present as parents. Participation in microenterprise programs has helped them maximize the financial return from their businesses and in many cases achieve access to credit, emotional support, help with legal and accounting matters, and other critical resources. More states need to work with microenterprise programs that target low-income people to help this group use self-employment as an exit strategy rather than placing obstacles in the way.

The programs that serve this population require greater funding for training and support than programs that serve a population with fewer barriers to success. In view of the characteristics of this target population, programs that serve it should not be judged by the same standards as those that do not. Staff members at all three programs claimed that serving the welfare population often requires more training and a higher number of hours of support. The Association for Enterprise Opportunity conference confirmed this finding.[7] Participants may be lacking in basic skills or self-esteem and self-confidence. Some programs, like Women's Initiative, have a staff person devoted to helping participants deal with matters that could compromise their ability to successfully pursue self-employment. The trainers and business consultants in all three programs spend an enormous amount of time both in the classroom and in one-on-one training both before and after participants have graduated. Some funders and policymakers are more interested in making grants or loans than in supporting the training, one-on-one, technical assistance, and mentoring programs that are critical to making successful entrepreneurs out of welfare recipients. Policymakers who want to support the microenterprise strategy for welfare recipients must invest in training.

Another critical point: there is an enormous need for jobs that provide benefits and pay a living wage. Self-employment is the best option for some welfare recipients, but it is the only option for too many. The demands of running a business are great for anyone, but for a low-income single parent, they can be overwhelming. Until good jobs are available to the poor, microenterprise programs that target these people and help them start and run solid businesses are providing a necessary service.

7. "Working with AFDC Recipients," session at the Association for Enterprise Opportunity Conference (AEO), Washington, D.C., April 1998. AEO is the trade association for U.S. microenterprise programs.

SIX   *Networking,*

           Social Capital, and

           Community Development

MICROENTERPRISE PROGRAMS clearly build social
capital, those "features of social organization, such as trust, norms, and
networks, that can improve the efficiency of society by facilitating coordinated actions."[1] These coordinated actions, in turn, build community.
Though just as important as creating jobs and generating income, community development is often overlooked, perhaps because the activities it
entails—training residents, helping them gain access to resources, and connecting them with each other and with critical organizations—are difficult to see and evaluate. This chapter looks closely at Women's Initiative
and Working Capital to determine how microenterprise programs develop
the networks that build community, to what extent the networks are embedded in program structure, and how network formation leads to the
accumulation of social capital.[2]

Microenterprise programs build two types of networks: those within
programs that typically involve borrowers, and those between programs
and other institutions. Intraprogram networks consist of the relationships
formed among borrowers and between borrowers and program staff.
Interprogram networks consist of the external links that programs make
with other community-based organizations as well as other institutions in
the public and private sectors.

1. Putnam (1993, p. 167).
2. The interaction between social capital and elements within credit associations has
been examined (Putnam 1993), but no one has looked specifically at the formation and
operation of these networks in U.S. programs.

Social Capital and the Importance of Networks

Although the concept of social capital has existed for many years, only recently has it become a central issue among those who work in community development and poverty alleviation. Reliable indicators of it have not yet been developed and tested. Some recent evidence suggests that it can take centuries to build.[3] Given that the microenterprise movement in this country is only a decade old, it is impossible to claim yet that these programs have produced lasting social capital. Yet there are some signs that social capital is being produced and that gains have been made in community development. The indicators are the relationships among people and organizations that have been created or strengthened as a result of the presence of a microenterprise program.

These relationships combine to form "networks of civic engagement [that] represent intense horizontal interaction. The denser such networks in a community, the more likely that its citizens will be able to cooperate for social benefit."[4] Social capital can provide two types of benefits: social leverage, which helps one "get ahead"; and social support, which helps one "get by."[5] The social capital that microenterprise programs produce falls into both categories; the social leverage component is especially important because many other networks that provide social leverage exclude disenfranchised groups.

The next section illustrates the intensity of intraprogram relationships. Currently, these networks are just beginning to spread across disadvantaged communities. The task now is to nurture them and make them more visible, and thereby to change these communities for the better.

Intraprogram Networks

The success of microenterprise programs arises in large part from the relationships among program participants.[6] The strength and quality of these relationships distinguish microenterprise programs both from mainstream

---

3. Putnam (1993).

4. Putnam (1993, p. 173).

5. Briggs (1998).

6. Servon (1997). Critical relationships are long-term bonds either between borrowers within a program or between borrowers and business consultants. The few programs that are extremely credit-driven, such as Accion US, are not nearly as dependent on these relationships as are the others, including those studied here.

financial institutions and from many other social welfare programs. On the surface, the relationships help ensure the payback of loans. But their other functions are arguably more important. Working Capital borrowers refer customers to each other; the regular group meetings also help to combat the isolation that many self-employed people experience. Women's Initiative borrowers receive broadly based support from business consultants who are sensitive to the complex needs of poor women. These relationships introduce motivated people into the networks that can help them gain access to previously inaccessible resources, from credit to mentoring.

Women's Initiative's Intraprogram Networks

To foster intraprogram relationships, Women's Initiative has found it helpful to focus on one group of people, namely women (see chapter 4).[7] According to Barbara Johnson, one of Women's Initiative's founders and its current executive director, women-only programs provide women with a unique opportunity to bond with each other. "Many women are very isolated from each other, especially if they are low income," she says. They may have been a part of "a lot of social institutions where they have the ability to make connections with other women such as church or . . . large extended families, but these also have a pretty defined role for women. And so women also need to be able to bond with other women in a different context, where they can identify themselves as other than dutiful wife, dutiful mother, good Christian."

The women interviewed were split about equally between those who were attracted to Women's Initiative specifically because it is a women's organization and those who came simply because it offered the services they needed. All of those interviewed believed that they had benefited from working with and learning from women once they began to participate. For many women, a women-only program builds trust more quickly. This trust is critical for extending the relationships beyond the program.

Although Women's Initiative serves women across the socioeconomic spectrum, the program targets those with a low income. To serve a population of this breadth, it must focus on training. Miriam Walden, the Women's Initiative loan fund manager, discussed the rationale underlying the programs philosophy:

7. Servon (1996).

We haven't gone out seeking folks that were already in a position to borrow. . . . Clearly Women's Initiative has chosen to work with a group of people who . . . require assistance in preparing their ability to argue for a loan and their ability to repay it. So that means you have to take on the training challenge in order to do it. . . . I think it's always been an expressed belief of this organization that people do not need money, they need training.

To work with a woman from the business idea stage to the borrowing stage there must also be a strong relationship between her and the business consultant.

In 1991 Women's Initiative began a program called WISESource in recognition of the benefits that entrepreneurs in the same industry could obtain by holding a forum to discuss common problems. Three groups currently meet, representing apparel and textiles, business services, and food. The groups include new entrepreneurs as well as those with experience. Members share information about suppliers, upcoming trade shows, and places to market their products. They also brainstorm to solve members' problems. The apparel and textiles group, which has been meeting for two years, has held holiday sales and shared booths at shows, along with registration, rental, and travel expenses. Anne, a Women's Initiative borrower who makes and sells high-end gift products out of hand-painted silk, told me that belonging to WISESource has given her "community."

It makes me feel more like a business person. . . . I didn't come here looking for that, but I'm really happy about that. Sometimes we meet outside of [Women's Initiative]. There's one person that's now a good friend. I consider her to be sort of a mentor. . . . She's a few steps ahead of me in business. It's been a struggle to stay together. We're all really busy but we all want to be here because we really need each other.

WISESource enables the program to continue to support clients who have already taken the program's courses or who find classes inappropriate, such as women who have been successful in their businesses for a long time but continue to feel isolated.

Although relationships among borrowers at Women's Initiative are important, the primary relationship is the one formed between a borrower and her business consultant. The heavy investment of time and holistic approach of Women's Initiative, which together build strong relationships, distinguish the business consultant–borrower relationship at Women's Initiative from lender-borrower relationships at other programs and at mainstream financial institutions. According to Karen Carter, a business consultant at Women's Initiative, "What we really do is to work on relationships. Today in banking, it's just paperwork. It's not about relationships. If you have any difficulty, they're not going to give you any consulting help."

Although both program staff and borrowers value this investment in relationships, it is also necessary from a practical perspective. Because the loans Women's Initiative makes are riskier than those made in mainstream financial institutions, relationships facilitate the kind of information gathering necessary for making lending decisions. Carter explained:

> Collateral is almost a joke. There's minimal collateral, somebody's TV. So in part we're banking on a relationship that's not strictly business but that gives us some sense of who this woman is. And if this woman has had all of these difficulties with her family and her children, but she's managed to hold it together, that's a character thing. Well, banks aren't asking about your character.

Johnson agrees: "When you look at the capital markets system in terms of where it's coming from . . . there is no recognition of the business idea, who is the person you're lending to, what has gone into all of that, all of the sweat equity, all of the know-how, all of the marketing." Walden adds a slightly different perspective to the relationships forged at Women's Initiative and how they differ from lender-borrower relationships at mainstream financial institutions:

> We're not making loans where there's already good business performance. Most of the loans we make, people can't perform well unless they grow. Where I think that banks tend to look at growth that has already happened, as evidenced by financial performance . . . most of the loans that we make are gambling on someone's ability to make future performance. And that's what drives the training. [If I don't] make them deal with the issues I'm identifying . . . then I don't get the loan money back.

At Women's Initiative, intangible assets such as trustworthiness, integrity, and dedication substitute for the hard assets, such as collateral, that determine creditworthiness in banks. These intangible assets can be fully assessed only if a strong and effective relationship is built between the borrower and her business consultant. Potential borrowers must complete fourteen weeks of classes before they are eligible for a loan.[8] During this time, the business consultant assesses both the solidity of the client's business idea and her personal readiness to pursue self-employment. The loan review committee (LRC) judges applications on the basis of the merit and feasibility of the business plan and the perceived drive and readiness of the applicant. Applicants often have troubled credit histories and no collateral; therefore, the relationship established in classes and in one-on-one meetings is critical. Sometimes a potential borrower is asked to do additional work or to stabilize her personal situation before applying for a loan.

Every borrower I interviewed described her relationship with her business consultant in similar terms. For all of them, the support went beyond getting the loan and surpassed their expectations. A critical aspect also seemed to be getting to a stage at which the borrower was not afraid to bring problems to the business consultant. Constance, who runs a talent booking agency, described her relationship with her business consultant:

> It's not just a lender/borrower thing. It's more like "I care about how you're doing, and what's going on, and how's your mental health." ... Or, "It looks like your business is slipping, here are some ideas you might want to think about." ... I couldn't imagine not having that sounding board. Miriam is fantastic. ... Like sometimes I'll say, "Miriam, I'm really stressed right now and I don't know if I can make these payments." And she'll just say, "Here's an idea—how about this, how about that. ..." And I think she would sooner do that than penalize me. There's just nothing else out there that has that kind of impact on me, except maybe my Mom.

Anne says that she has gotten to the point with her business consultant where, "I can come in and cry and say, 'I don't understand this cash flow stuff!' And she'll just say, 'Okay, let's just go through it again.' And so I've felt like it was okay to do that." Jill, an artist who designs and sells greeting cards, echoed this feeling of tremendous support: "I know that I can call up here if I want to any time during business hours and ask any question I need to." At the same time she recognized that it was not completely unconditional. "You have to be at that place. You have to really move

---

8. The exception is Women's Initiative's small first loans of up to $500 for clients who need funds to do test marketing or to develop a prototype of their product. Clients who are enrolled but have not yet completed classes are eligible for these loans.

yourself to get there," she said. "You come here with your inspiration, your product, your company, whatever, and enough to get you here, and then there's enough energy throughout the organization that keeps you— you know, you can put your stuffing back in."

The fact that Women's Initiative's mission extends beyond the simple act of making loans tends to muddy the relationship, however. As Walden puts it,

> The fact that we're not just out to make loans but that we're interested in developing businesses and people makes things hard. Because we have to say, "I'm not saying this because I'm a lender, I'm saying it because this is your business and I care about its ability to succeed, and it's my job to care about what its ability to succeed is and not just my job to decide whether or not to give you a loan." And that's just real hard for people to figure, and it confuses a lot of issues. It's really hard for us. . . . How much of our process is designed to help us decide whether we're in or out, and how much of our process is designed to help the client decide whether or not to borrow? . . . And so we sort of rock back and forth across this blurry, blurry line, and that confuses a lot of the relationships.

Women's Initiative's holistic approach to achieving its mission sometimes conflicts with what it means to be a lender. The fact that the same business consultant must simultaneously embody the desire to empower and the need to control causes these roles and responsibilities to be continually renegotiated.

Despite their complexity, the relationships Women's Initiative forms among borrowers and between borrowers and business consultants create connections where none previously existed. These relationships provide disenfranchised women with access to tangible resources such as credit and training, and intangibles such as support and role models. In short, they provide both social support and social leverage. Coupled with the interprogram relationships, these connections are the building blocks of community development.

Working Capital's Intraprogram Relationships

Working Capital works through community-based organizations (CBOs), called affiliates. The program typically approaches CBOs that it believes will make good affiliates on the basis of their capacity and connections with residents. The affiliate agrees to devote at least one staff person to the program's activities, and Working Capital trains the person to become an enterprise agent. Enterprise agents help coordinate the activities of Working Capital, the affiliate, and the borrowing groups. Enterprise agents run orientations, help get groups started, provide initial training, and monitor groups as they proceed through training and borrowing phases.

Borrowing and lending activities at Working Capital take place in the borrowing, or peer group (see chapter 4). The typical procedure in forming a group is as follows. The local affiliate holds an orientation session to explain how the Working Capital program works. The sessions also bring together local entrepreneurs who, because they often work out of their homes, are invisible in their communities. During this initial meeting, those who are interested in forming a group talk about their businesses and their interests. Entrepreneurs decide for themselves how comfortable they are with the others. Sometimes an entrepreneur will attend more than one orientation session before finding others with a similar vision. Others may join a group and drop out if they are uncomfortable with the way the group functions.

Group members, with some help from their enterprise agent, meet regularly (usually once a month) to progress through the training materials, become chartered, and accept or deny each other's loan applications. The peer group structure is the primary vehicle by which Working Capital builds intraprogram networks.

Peer group lending uses small groups (usually between three and ten members) to provide training and credit. Members may or may not know each other before joining. They undergo training together and submit applications for loans, which are reviewed by the entire group. The group extends credit to members that have met whatever requirements the program or other group members set. Members may continue to apply for and receive credit only as long as all members remain current on their payments. If one falls behind or defaults, the others must cover the unpaid balance. Because all group members are effectively cosigners for all other group members, they have a strong incentive to work together and to ensure, to the extent possible, that businesses are sound before they agree to lend to them. In some programs that use peer lending, borrowers also pay into an emergency fund that can be used to cover a late payment or, for example, to help a group member get through a difficult time. Some programs require group members to establish a savings program.

The peer-lending methodology serves both philosophical and practical purposes. On the philosophical side, the fact that borrowers make all the lending decisions together helps to empower them. In addition, because members both lend to and borrow from one another, the hierarchical borrowing structure embodied in mainstream financial institutions is leveled. Most important—from the standpoint of community development—because group members meet regularly even after they have completed training and regardless of whether each member is currently making loan payments, the group helps build social capital in other ways. Members network, share information, bring problems to one another, and set goals together.

On the practical side, this structure helps minimize operating costs, which is particularly important given the small size of the loans. Peer lending also creates networks of people who learn to trust each other within communities that need more than individual empowerment. The businesses that Working Capital serves are often home-based, part-time, sole proprietorships, making them hard to locate and serve. The group structure renders these businesses visible both to other Working Capital entrepreneurs and to the communities in which these entrepreneurs operate.

Once a group is formed, members proceed through the six stages outlined in table 6-1. Group members first learn about each other and each other's businesses. They also choose a name for the group—one group was named First Class Entrepreneurs—and this name lays the foundation for cooperation and unity. The process of choosing a name forces members to think about and focus on what they have in common. The next stage involves training. With the help of their enterprise agent, members proceed through business training exercises and learn how to evaluate each other's loan applications. During stage three the groups elect officers—chairperson, treasurer, and secretary—and write bylaws. The bylaws govern all aspects of group participation. They specify conditions of membership, loan approval, and the course of action to be taken in case of default. The only rule that Working Capital imposes on groups is that all members must be current in their payments before any member can proceed to the next loan level.

Stages four and five of the group lending process focus on actual lending. Group members submit applications and discuss them with the rest of the group. The group then decides whether to approve or reject the application. Checks are distributed and repayment begins. If the group is not confident in a member's business sense or creditworthiness, members generally propose a plan for the member to follow to achieve readiness. In

Table 6-1. *Stages of Group Lending Process*

Stage	Description
1	Discuss each other's business and personal profiles; choose a group name.
2	Practice income statement exercise and loan application process.
3	Write group bylaws and elect officers.
4	Train officers; review and approve or reject loan applications.
5	Distribute checks and celebrate.
6	Develop six-month action plan.

one group, when members were uncomfortable with one member's weak reading and writing skills, two members volunteered to tutor him. They made improved literacy a prerequisite for reapplication. Each group's by-laws typically spell out a process for dismissing group members who do not meet the standards set by the group, but these differ from one group to the next. A 1994 study commissioned by Working Capital and conducted by Mt. Auburn Associates found very high satisfaction with the various elements of the group process. Table 6-2 illustrates the findings. Perhaps the most significant was that for groups to be effective, "there must be a mutual commitment to the success of group members and a willingness to support one another and solve problems through the group process. . . . The group must not be viewed as simply a means to obtain capital."[9]

The peer-lending process creates strong relationships among group members. Although enterprise agents link borrowers to the main program in a manner reminiscent of that of the Women's Initiative business consultant, the enterprise agent's role is a much diminished relative of the business consultant. This is a deliberate strategy, intended to enable Working Capital to attain its overarching goal: to empower *groups* of borrowers. This process motivates participants to help themselves and each other, to grow as a unit, and to extend that growth beyond the group.

The fact that the program works through community organizations/affiliates has produced both heterogeneous groups and others that are united by some common bond. Peter, a plasterer and contractor, belongs to a group that is very mixed across gender, racial, and ethnic lines. He did not know the people in the group before joining but said that because all

9. Mt. Auburn Associates (1994, p. 5).

Table 6-2. *Satisfaction with Group Process*
Percent

Activity	Very satisfied	Somewhat satisfied	Somewhat dissatisfied	Very dissatisfied	N^a
Writing bylaws	72.8	23.4	2.5	1.3	158
Reviewing loans	70.2	21.8	7.3	0.7	151
Resolving dis- agreements	75.5	11.1	10.4	3.0	135
Handling late payments	67.8	20.0	7.8	4.4	90

Source: Mt. Auburn Associates (1994).
a. Excludes "not applicable" responses.

of them are business people any potential problems that may have arisen from cultural differences have been eliminated. Richard, a computer consultant who works part-time at his business, joined a Spanish-speaking group, partly because he wanted to target his computer consulting services to Latino businesses and he recognized the networking potential of participating in Working Capital. Because he no longer lives or works in the Spanish-speaking community, this group also allows Richard to practice his Spanish. Nina's group is made up solely of women, one of whom is her sister-in-law. Although Nina, who bakes and sells cakes out of her home, says that it was not their goal to form a women's group, its makeup has allowed the members to address issues such as the problem of being young and a woman and not being taken seriously in the business world. Nina says: "One of the things that held me back is just that fear that because I'm black, because I'm a woman, because I'm young they're [traditional lending agencies] not going to take me seriously." Joining Working Capital and talking about these problems with the other women in her group has been helpful.

The Mt. Auburn study found that several effective groups were composed of people who faced similar challenges to economic success. According to the study, "Such groups develop a commitment to mutual support based on their common experiences and objectives."[10] Through its affiliates, Working Capital can target many disenfranchised groups efficiently; the affiliates, with their combination of closeness to the commu-

10. Mt. Auburn Associates (1994, p. 5).

nity and Working Capital training, have the expertise to tailor the basic approach to the specific needs of the people they serve. Working Capital does not have to acquire this knowledge to reach these populations. In addition, the fact that many of the groups are as heterogeneous as Peter's may operate to break down harmful stereotypes that can operate even in small communities.

Not surprisingly, the benefits borrowers talk about when asked what impact the program has had on their lives and on their businesses are directly related to belonging to the group. Credit and training are mentioned secondarily, if at all. According to Nelson Quintero, who works with Working Capital's New Bedford, Massachusetts, affiliate,

> The impact [of the program on borrowers] has basically been in the educational part, in being able to work together as a group, being able to share information and referrals, in the workshops and consultations. That's where the impact is. It's not the money. The money's not even close. It's coming together and negotiating and conducting business in that environment, things that a lot of people have not been exposed to.

Indeed, the two words that borrowers mention over and over when talking about the benefits of participating in Working Capital are "support" and "networking."[11] With respect to general support, nearly all borrowers discussed the benefits of getting together with other small business owners to talk about common problems. Joyce, who works long hours alone at her upholstery business, described her group as "an extended sort of family, folks with almost the same problems." She continued: "When we get together we'll, you know, certain things we'll discuss. Then we realize one of us may have had that problem before, so it's easy to tell the other one that this is how you go about it. So it's good therapy. Very good therapy. . . . You feel good going to the meetings, and you feel even better when you leave there."

Richard also used the concept of family to describe what goes on in his group. He believes that this sense of family results in part from working

---

11. The women I interviewed were much more inclined to emphasize the supportive aspect of their groups, while the men were more likely to stress the networking opportunities program participation provided. Although the number of interviews I conducted does not allow me to make sweeping conclusions based on this observation, it is supported by focus groups conducted as part of Working Capital's recent evaluation.

closely with other members over a long period of time. "It's nurturing and there's helping, and sometimes you need to be pushed and sometimes you're . . . pulling someone yourself." Several participants also discussed the isolating aspect of being self-employed and how belonging to the group has functioned to mitigate that isolation. Marian, who runs her cleaning business out of her home, said: "Being self-employed can be very lonely, and it's . . . almost like therapy when you get together and you hear that other people are experiencing this. . . .You just know you're not in it alone." Betty's group helped her to take the step of leaving her job to pursue her balloon business full time. She said that her group had given her "the courage . . . to be a business-oriented person. . . . "They basically said, 'Look. You're either going to have to jump in and hold your nose or jump in and sink. . . .We had to do the same thing.' So here I am."

All of the borrowers interviewed described both the group meetings and larger events such as the annual trade show as great information-sharing and networking opportunities. These activities function both to help the internal operations of the businesses and to expand the range of their marketing efforts. For example, Marian hired the son of one of her group members to work in her cleaning business. She also found a tax lawyer through another group member. One of Betty's group members is spending extra time with her outside of the regular meetings to help her write her business plan.

In Herb's group, each member keeps business cards of other members to hand out when opportunities arise. When people ask him about the program, he emphasizes the potential for networking:

> There's a lot of networking that happens that you need as a business. Free advertising, man. That's what I tell them. You know? I went to a conference with eighty other businesses . . . and there were so many different businesses going on there, and I met this guy and I met that guy and I met this woman and I met that woman and she's the head of this and she's got my card and she asked for my profile. You know? How else could I pay for that?

Although Manfred believes his business has outgrown what Working Capital can provide in terms of credit, he plans to stay involved to benefit from the networking. "I've networked a lot through Working Capital," he says. Even when he stops borrowing, he says, "I'll still attend all the meetings, and it's good to be connected." Others have gotten business directly from Working Capital contacts. Joyce has reupholstered furniture for several of her group members. Betty did the balloon work for a party that one of her group members threw. The business that they get from group members exposes them to other potential customers. The majority of the borrowers I interviewed obtain most of their business through word of mouth.

According to Kim Wilson, the creation of networks that begins at the level of the individual group fosters Working Capital's economic development goals:

> We're really colonizing markets that were previously invisible because these people were in their homes. They were tucked away in various parts. Now they're brought out into these groups, and they're reachable . . . And now that they're reachable, they've got addresses, we can reach group chairs, we can organize things.

Once formed, these networks can act as the conduit for many activities.

An overwhelming number of the borrowers interviewed expressed an intent to use their business to give back to the community, and one has already begun to put his intentions into practice. The ways the entrepreneurs plan to do this, or are doing it already, vary from one individual to the next, but nearly all have clearly thought about the role their business plays in the community. Joyce's expansion plans include teaching the upholstery trade to young women "who may not want to go to college or they may get into trouble." Joyce's logic is that "rather than end up on welfare the rest of their life, they can learn a trade with me and be self-sufficient. So that's one of my plans, and . . . it's in the works right now, so I'm going to need every loan I can get my hands on."

Richard also wants to hire and train inner-city youth once he is able to pursue his business full time. Herb, a building contractor and estimator, already employs two interns from Youth Build who were high school dropouts and had been in trouble with the law. He says that after working with him for a month, one of the interns expressed a desire to run his own business. According to Herb, the intern said, "You know, I never knew that black men had businesses like this." Manfred, who claims that "the bottom line is that we're for profit," also plans to establish an education fund for his employees, all of whom are young people from his neighborhood, and to donate 5 percent of his profits to the fund. "I see what's happening. I've had many friends in jail and many friends killed. . . . I grew up really with not much, and I just want to give it back." Programs like Working Capital function not only to help very small businesses succeed but also to create the opportunity for this kind of benefit to be realized.

Working Capital's goal of organizing these entrepreneurs into a strong and visible network brings ideas such as these much closer to reality. The network building of the organization can serve a variety of purposes. It begins with helping the entrepreneurs gain access to the services they need. They also get support and additional marketing by becoming visible to each other. They may use their organization to pressure those in power for change. And finally, their visibility can help others.

It is impossible to know how Working Capital has fostered community orientation. Are community-minded entrepreneurs drawn to participate in Working Capital because of its group structure, focus on organizing, and link to existing community development corporations? Or does the networking that occurs in groups motivate this kind of response? It seems likely that the answer to both questions is yes. Program staff member Marcy Goldstein-Gelb tells a story about an information meeting in Dorchester that illustrates the catalytic potential of Working Capital:

> We had about thirty people. And the entrepreneur was describing the program, and some of the businesses said, "Wait a minute. What happens? We're responsible for each other? What happens if this happens?" And people started asking questions and becoming concerned. And then this guy stood up and said, "This is our opportunity to take back our community. How often do we get a chance to really build our own businesses and buy from each other and work with each other and have a say in . . . decisions that count?" And all of a sudden the entire room just—the tenor just changed. They said "Yeah! This is our community! We're going to have a say and we're going to be able to do this and that!" And that's to me what is exciting. That's what we do well, because just by virtue of simply bringing people together and by telling them, "You're going to make the decisions." That's enough. That's a start.

Working Capital operates from the assumption that this community mindedness exists in disadvantaged areas. Without opportunities such as those the program provides, this energy remains too diffused to make change happen.

In many Working Capital communities, doing community work begins with the formation of a borrowers' council. According to Sarah Smith, a VISTA volunteer who works with the program, these councils, started by

Table 6-3. *Positive Impact of Working Capital Participation on Professional and Personal Life*

Percent

Category of impact	A lot	Some	Little	None	N
Commitment to the business	39.7	34.6	10.3	15.4	156
Self-confidence	41.7	32.1	12.2	14.1	154
Participation in civic or social activities outside the group	19.5	24.7	16.9	39.0	154
Family relationships	14.9	18.2	13.0	53.9	154

Source: Mt. Auburn Associates (1994).

the borrowers, consist of representatives of several groups. Smith says that a borrowers' council is "sort of a forum where they can discuss issues related to their businesses, to Working Capital in general. They can plan networking events, fund-raisers, maybe plan to support a local candidate, whatever they decide." Having had some experience with the networking that goes on in their own groups, the borrowers who form these councils want to extend this activity to the whole program. These borrowers' councils are also figuring out ways to meet other needs. In New Bedford, for example, the council has created a buffer fund to cover loan payments for members who are unable to meet their loan obligations. Through these councils, Smith says, "borrowers themselves are recognizing the different needs they have and are taking the initiative to make some changes."

The Mt. Auburn study supports the view that participation in Working Capital causes participants to become more involved in their communities. Nearly 20 percent of respondents reported that participating in Working Capital had "a lot" of impact on their participation in civic or social activities outside the group, and 14.9 percent claimed that participation had "a lot" of impact on their family relationships. Table 6-3 illustrates other nonfinancial aspects of participant well-being reported in this study. Working Capital participants attribute many effects on their professional and personal lives to participation in the program. These statistics support the hypothesis that there are interactions between running a successful business and more tangential variables such as self-confidence, family stability, and belonging to community networks.

The Working Capital mission states that the program uses groups to build communities of people who have little other access to the resources needed to earn a living such as credit and training. The processes of learning, cooperating, and trust-building that are incorporated into the peer group structure lay the foundation for the networking, community organizing, and creation of a critical mass of small businesses that constitute some of Working Capital's goals. The credit helps get people in the door. The decisionmaking they have to do as part of a group—whether or not they themselves borrow—is empowering because it gives them greater control over their own lives and businesses and over their community through the act of working with and helping others.

Interprogram Networks

In recent years the field of community development has focused increasingly on networking among programs as a way to build capacity and serve the constituents of community-based organizations more comprehensively.[12] This movement toward networking came about because CBOs recognized the interconnectedness of various social problems and because of cuts in government funding. Networking is one way for the organizations to do more with less.

Networking between organizations is not a new phenomenon in the microenterprise world. Because of the array of services small business owners need, most microenterprise programs have long histories of forming relationships with other institutions. The types of organizations and institutions with which microenterprise programs typically enter relationships include banks, other private sector corporations, funders, churches, community colleges, other microenterprise programs, community-based organizations, and government agencies at the local, state, and federal levels.

The relationships that microenterprise programs enter into—particularly with mainstream institutions such as banks and private corporations—alter norms within these institutions. For example, many banks that contribute to microenterprise loan funds begin to lend to a wider population after learning more, through their work with the programs, about borrowers' bankability and commitment to their businesses. Like the trust building that occurs in intraprogram relationships, the alter-

---

12. Harrison and Cordero-Guzman (1996).

ation of attitudes and practices that occurs in interprogram relationships builds social capital.

Interprogram relationships can be contractual or casual. They are also distinguished by the importance of the microenterprise program in the relationship. For the purposes of this discussion, networks include both formal and informal ties that bridge boundaries across organizations, localities, or competencies.[13]

Bennett Harrison and Hector Cordero-Guzman have identified three types of community development networks that have bearing on this analysis: hub-spoke, peer-to-peer, and intermediary networks.[14] In hub-spoke networks, the CBO holds a central, initiating position. Peer-to-peer networks are characterized by a lack of one dominant, central organization. Intermediary networks involve a non-CBO entity such as a community college or community development collaborative that takes the lead in forming the network. Working Capital is the hub in its network of banks, CBOs, and other institutions; WISE generally engages in peer-to-peer network relationships.

Women's Initiative's Interprogram Networks

The relationships that Women's Initiative enters into are usually less formal and more peer-to-peer than those catalyzed by Working Capital. The programs' structure is far less dependent on interprogram relationships than is the structure of Working Capital. The relationships that Women's Initiative enters into broaden and deepen the services that the program already provides. The peer-to-peer structure of the networks, however, does not diminish the importance of the relationships within it. In fact, as a program that is better established and more mature than many others, Women's Initiative is often asked to participate in partnerships. Barbara Johnson believes that people approach Women's Initiative in part because it is "a successful, visible program," and being associated with it "will help add credence to their program."

Several relationships have been critical to Women's Initiative's operations from the beginning. The program was founded in 1986 as a sponsored project of the San Francisco Women's Foundation, a relationship that gave Women's Initiative entry into an established network of women's

13. Harrison and Cordero-Guzman (1996).
14. Harrison and Cordero-Guzman (1996).

organizations and CBOs in the Bay Area. After having been sponsored by the Women's Foundation for nearly two years, Women's Initiative was launched as a separate nonprofit organization in October 1988. Two relationships that were critical at that point and remain important today are links with the San Francisco Mayor's Office on Community Development (MOCD) and Bank of America.

In 1986 MOCD created Self-Employment and Entrepreneurship Development (SEED), a special initiative to fund self-employment in San Francisco. MOCD funds SEED with federal Community Development Block Grant (CDBG) funds. Women's Initiative is one of the four programs supported by the SEED program. SEED links Women's Initiative both to city government and to other San Francisco-based microenterprise programs. According to Johnson, the inclusion of Women's Initiative in SEED was "a lucky break because there was a new director who was looking for ways to fill the gaps . . . and we fit that perfectly. It was very good timing."

Bank of America fulfills some of its Community Reinvestment Act requirements by helping Women's Initiative with operating expenses—early on in the form of office space and telephone service and currently in funds specifically designated for rent and phones. This early relationship with the bank has also helped Women's Initiative forge relationships with other Bay Area banks. Women's Initiative has established itself in the community to the extent that banks call the program and refer customers who appear to need additional work before obtaining a loan.

Women's Initiative has also forged a successful relationship with local Small Business Administration (SBA) officials. If a woman needs a loan exceeding the maximum limit set by Women's Initiative, her business consultant can work to secure an SBA loan through a third-tier bank. With these relatively large ($50,000 or $60,000) loans, the advocacy of the Women's Initiative business consultant on behalf of the borrower opens access to credit that the borrower would not have been able to achieve on her own. According to Helen Branham, director of Women's Initiative's Oakland office, "There's a lot of credibility that goes along with a referral that comes to a banker from us because they have gone through our training program and they have developed a business plan, they have some insight into what makes a business successful. That really helps their chances." This three-way relationship between a nonprofit organization, a for-profit corporation, and a government agency illustrates the benefits that can accrue from well-chosen interprogram relationships. Women's Initiative also operates as an intermediary through the SBA Women's Pilot

Demonstration and Low-Doc programs, making Women's Initiative eligible to qualify women for SBA loans through them.[15]

The most formal partnership Women's Initiative has entered into was with the Bay Area Women's Resource Center (BAWRC) to offer intensive services to homeless women. Sponsored by the Roberts Foundation and begun in 1991, this project was originally called the Homeless Women's Economic Development Project (HWEDP) and, later, SF WEST. During the years that it operated, it admitted about ten women each year and provided them with individual and group counseling, business training and credit, housing, transportation, and child care. The premise of the project was that some homeless women, given the right kind of support, can attain economic independence through self-employment. This project, while much more costly per participant than the main program, tested the microenterprise strategy on a very difficult population. It also demonstrated the benefits that can be accrued through creating relationships between programs that offer different but compatible services.

Recognizing the high demand for self-employment services in the East Bay, particularly Oakland, Women's Initiative opened an Oakland office in November 1993. Helen Branham notes that "an original part of our design actually was to establish relationships with the other community economic development entities in order to impact the community for the women we serve." The Oakland branch is located in a building that has been designated the one-stop capital shop for the City of Oakland. Other entities housed in the same building include the Small Business Development Center and the Oakland Small Business Development Corporation. Branham has also established a relationship with the Oakland Economic Development and Employment Department, which brokers services for entrepreneurs and routes them to places like Women's Initiative where they can obtain the services they need.

The Women's Initiative Oakland office also participates in the City of Oakland's HUD-funded HOPE 6 project, which has been operating for three years.[16] Most of the HOPE programs that have been initiated nationwide focus on housing. According to Colin Lacon, who administers HOPE 6 in Oakland, the Oakland effort is unusual in that it has allocated

---

15. Low-Doc stands for low documentation. The program is designed to decrease the bureaucracy and paperwork of the lending process, making it easier for people to borrow.

16. HOPE stands for Housing Opportunities for People Everywhere. HOPE 6 is the sixth such effort funded by the Department of Housing and Urban Development.

the maximum amount of the grant possible to nonhousing activities. Lacon explains that Oakland organizers began with the assumption that "if you don't support the people, build capacity within people, it doesn't help just to fix up the place, the place just deteriorates." The City of Oakland recruited twelve community-based organizations to join the effort. The main benefit that Women's Initiative gets from this program is a strong link both to the city and to other participating CBOs. According to Branham,

> if a woman comes to us and she definitely is interested in starting a business but in order to start one she needs money for transportation ... and she also needs child care, then what we would do is refer that woman to her eligibility worker at the Oakland Housing Authority and/or the Department of Social Services, and then we would find her the resources that could help support those needs in order to participate in our program.

The HOPE 6 partners meet regularly to talk about issues that affect program success. This program has forged a strong network of CBOs in Oakland, and the network helps programs to serve constituents more completely.

The equivalent of the HOPE 6 program in the San Francisco office is the Women Mean Business program. Barbara Johnson believes that a microenterprise program like Women's Initiative that serves poor people is a natural candidate for partnerships with other organizations. Women's Initiative cannot meet all the needs of its clients. The Women Mean Business program formalizes the responsibility of referral. Women Mean Business, which is funded through the Job Opportunities for Low-Income Individuals (JOLI) program of the U.S. Department of Health and Human Services, works with the segment of Women's Initiative's target population that needs such additional services as child care, housing assistance, and personal effectiveness training. The process of formalizing referral relationships with other area organizations has created strong connections between Women's Initiative and other CBOs. According to Gail Spann-Lawson, who administers the Women Mean Business Program,

> We're getting calls from other agencies who are making referrals, thinking about us and thinking about how we might benefit their clients and vice versa and that's the whole idea behind this because at any number of the things that I've done, the staff people say, "I'm really glad you came out because now we know what you do. We do

get women in here that ask about starting a business and most of the time they end up walking away [thinking] that's not something they could ever do."

Spann-Lawson believes that the element of human connection built into Women Mean Business greatly enhances the interorganization relationships.

Private funders have also been important in Women's Initiative's ability to forge interprogram relationships. The James Irvine Foundation, a major funder of microenterprise programs, provided early multiyear support for four women-only microenterprise programs in California: Women's Initiative, Los Angeles–based Coalition for Women's Economic Development, the WEST Enterprise Center in Ukiah, and Women's Economic Growth in Weed. Irvine called these four programs the Women's Economic Development Initiative (WEDI) and required them to meet regularly to share information and problem-solving strategies. As a result of this early collaboration, the WEDI programs later formed the California Association for Microenterprise Opportunity, a coalition of microenterprise programs and other sympathetic institutions that collects information and works for change at the state level of government to create a political environment more compatible with these programs' missions.

Despite the generally positive experiences Women's Initiative has had in its work with other organizations, Barbara Johnson believes that "no partnership is trouble free . . . because of the different missions but the same populations that we're working with." Some conflict is inevitable, and organizations with limited resources like Women's Initiative must think long and hard about what they gain from entering into these relationships. At the same time, deeper government funding cuts mean that all nonprofit organizations must do more with less, and partnerships will become more attractive. Johnson thinks that the partnerships Women's Initiative has formed with other nonprofits are easier to negotiate than those formed with government agencies because the agencies tend to have more power over these nonprofits and less accountability to them.

> The recognition from the government sector and the understanding of what it takes to do this is really, really insufficient and very much impacted by historical standards of job training and assisting welfare dependent individuals to get off welfare. . . . We know how the success rates of those have been, but they are still using those numbers and they're just not comparable. So that's a problem. I've also

seen when a local or state program is starting to be put together, they go and look up what the Feds have done, what were the criteria the EDA used? Nobody wants to recreate a wheel, nobody wants to state a new definition, to substantiate something creative.

At the same time, "most of what any organization that's involved in a partnership is invested in is what do I get, what do my clients get from this relationship." She emphasizes that it is the actual relationships that make networks work, much more than the specific physical information that flows between organizations. "That's what a partnership is, a relationship," she says. "Many times it's the informal relationships that make it happen."

Johnson believes that because friction and conflict enter into relationships between organizations as a matter of course, they must be addressed explicitly, particularly in the current environment of decreasing resources. To try to find "specific ways to break that competitiveness, that lack of working together and to build ways to trust, to build a political camaraderie," Johnson and fifteen other representatives of Bay Area CBOs have formed the Community Institute. The purpose of this organization is to build a strong enough constituency to affect policy and resources. To do that, Johnson says, "there has got to be a very big trust level and a very big capacity ability, peer to peer." Although this work is important, most of the people involved are already overextended in their commitments to their own organizations and progress is necessarily slow.

The relationships Women's Initiative forms with banks, government agencies, and other CBOs illustrate the peer-to-peer model. Women's Initiative sometimes initiates these relationships and sometimes is invited to participate by another organization. In most cases, no single organization dominates, and the perceived benefits derived are beneficial for all.

Working Capital's Interprogram Networks

Interprogram networking is a much more explicit part of the Working Capital model than of Women's Initiative and has been from the beginning. Because the emphasis is on working through existing community organizations and depending on area banks, the potential for community development is built into the program. The FINCA model (see chapters 2 and 4) that founder Jeff Ashe adapted for Working Capital stresses a decentralized way of operating. This element was attractive to Ashe because it helps keep program costs down. As Marcy Goldstein-Gelb, who has been with the program since its inception, points out, it taps into existing resources such as the business training already offered through other organizations.

Working Capital does its lending through existing organizations, which, as mentioned earlier, are called affiliates. These can be community-based groups, local human services agencies, or government agencies. Working Capital looks for organizations that have strong community ties and that demonstrate a commitment to the methods and mission of the program.

Affiliates also provide Working Capital with immediate entry into their local networks. The attachment of Working Capital to another CBO gives the program legitimacy and credibility without having to spend years building trust in the community. In New Bedford, Massachusetts, Working Capital pairs with People Acting in Community Endeavors (PACE), and this relationship has helped PACE become involved in economic development work that the city desperately needs. William Maddocks, director of development for PACE, finds that becoming a Working Capital affiliate,

> made a significant change on the organization. It got us involved in a whole area of looking at providing services and advocacy for low-income, working-class clients that are connected to the agency that are people that maybe wouldn't have been connected with the agency—an area that we would not have or hadn't intended to get involved in—so it's kind of opened up the doors to the agency becoming much more involved in the broader economic development issue. . . . We've lost about 12,000 or 15,000 manufacturing jobs in this city in the last eight years, so taking a role in terms of economic development has been important for us.

PACE's extension into economic development work has motivated the organization to form relationships with banks, political organizations, and private businesses.

The availability of Working Capital services has attracted a broader range of people to PACE. Bringing higher-income people into the organization may have beneficial spillover effects if those drawn by Working Capital begin to work on other projects. With this very idea in mind, PACE recently created a Progress Panel, which consists of the leaders of all borrowing groups. The panel focuses partly on the internal functioning of groups and partly on creating networking opportunities for members of loan groups to meet each other. This networking has led borrowers to participate in a community coalition called Civic, which concentrates on political work such as making microenterprise development a campaign issue and educating politicians and others about why microentrepreneurs need more support. Civic is an organization made up of neighborhood resident organizations, and Working Capital is just one member of this group. Maddocks believes that the alliance with Civic has enabled the New Bedford Working Capital program to have a political impact as well as an economic one. In addition, PACE may not have been able to achieve these gains without Working Capital.

In Lawrence, an older industrial city thirty-five miles north of Boston, the Working Capital affiliate is the Lawrence Minority Business Council (LMBC). Nelson Quintero, a member of the executive committee and board of directors, indicates the council does a great deal of work with other community groups "to help them organize themselves so they can come together in economies of scale." LMBC currently works with the Taxi Association, the Latino Professional Association, a grocers' association, and a hair stylists' association. These relationships strengthen the network on which borrowers rely.

Operating expenses for Working Capital are financed primarily by grants from public agencies and philanthropic institutions. The loan fund, however, comes largely from banks in the form of lines of credit. Some banks also provide loan processing services and operating grants. These relationships expand the program's potential funding base and get banks involved in lending to a population with which they have previously had little contact. Banks benefit by expanding their market—they may become the next lender for businesses that graduate from Working Capital—and, in some cases, by fulfilling CRA requirements. Historically, the banks have not served this population because the loans are too small to make a sufficient profit and because the loans were considered too risky. Working Capital, through its technical assistance and group lending structure, minimizes the risk. In addition, a loan-loss reserve pool financed by the MacArthur Foundation serves as a credit enhancement to the bank lines. Working Capital's repayment rate of 95 percent demonstrates that the risk is much more perceived than actual.

Although cost-effectiveness has been a big concern within Working Capital in comparison with other microenterprise programs, lending to this population obviously remains unprofitable for banks. However, in a move that signals that Working Capital really has begun to alter the mindset of the banks with which it works, one bank recently offered to become both the affiliate and lender in its region, effectively offering to support the Working Capital program from within the bank.[17] Other banks have offered to extend credit automatically to borrowers who have been active for two years with Working Capital. And some banks have agreed to expand their participation beyond simply funding lending activities. "The role of the banks," says Goldstein-Gelb, "has evolved significantly." The operating support banks provide, she points out, is much more important than their contributions to the loan pool. Funders have typically been more inclined to contribute to microenterprise programs' loan funds than to their operating budgets. This tendency arises out of a fundamental misunderstanding of how U.S. microenterprise programs operate. Access to credit is a critical part of what these programs do, but getting potential borrowers to the point of readiness to borrow generally requires a level of training and hand-holding that is expensive. Funders often erroneously believe that microenterprise programs are inexpensive. The programs must therefore work hard to educate banks and other funders about how much the programs do. "We have banks that have sponsored communities or have sponsored some of our training materials, and so . . . a really important part of building the program is keeping the banks involved," Goldstein-Gelb says.

After recognizing that some of its borrowers needed greater financing than Working Capital could provide, LMBC worked with seven area banks to develop a spin-off second-tier microloan program that begins lending at $5,000. These seven banks, notes Nelson Quintero,

> saw the success of Working Capital, how we had developed the program, the number of participants involved, and saw that there was a . . . gap between $5,000 and $25,000. Community Development [an agency of the City of Lawrence] has something called the Small Business Development Loan Fund and that starts at $5,000 and goes up to $50,000. So there was a gap between $5,000 and $25,000 and that's where the idea of putting this second-tier loan program came from. There were individuals who knew of Working Capital, knew of the Minority Business Council, but at the same time knew that we couldn't meet their needs because they were beyond $5,000.

The relationships between LMBC and the area banks have also taught the banks a great deal about alternative lending criteria. Since the first

---

17. When I completed my fieldwork, Working Capital was still negotiating an appropriate arrangement with this bank.

two groups initiated this second-tier program, Quintero says, there have been changes in

> the amount of documentation that was involved, things having to do with their credit history. Basically, it came down to the fact that the criteria that were used to lend money—commercial loans on the street—were being used in the second tier. The only difference was that [LMBC borrowers] were receiving a smaller amount, they were in a group, and they were receiving technical assistance. Other than that there was no difference, so we made some changes to make it more of a character loan, meaning that credit history would still be looked at, but things like bankruptcy could be explained and if there was a legitimate reason for that bankruptcy, that would be taken into account. When we started out, anybody with a bankruptcy in their report was automatically out.

This example illustrates how Working Capital affiliates can use their success as a springboard to develop relationships with banks that open up greater access to capital. Ultimately, these kinds of relationships produce more community economic development than either the program alone could have produced or than would have been produced in the absence of Working Capital altogether.

As the hub in its hub-spoke network of interprogram relationships, Working Capital acts as the node that links other organizations to itself and to each other. Speaking about the work the program has done in Boston, Jeff Ashe explained: "It pulled together a lot of disparate organizations into a common initiative, a common program. So, where the organizations tend to be quite competitive or just not deal with each other at all, each totally isolated, this program tends to bring them together in an integrated effort." The work that the program does to connect organizations also helps some of them become stronger entities. Ashe illustrates this with the example of the Working Capital affiliate in Lawrence. "The Minority Business Council went from almost nothing to being a very strong, respected, lead organization in the city . . . mostly because of their interaction with Working Capital."

Trust, Norms, and Networks

The relationships formed between microenterprise programs and other organizations and institutions can help them link program participants to critical services without having to gain expertise in an entirely new area. Potential microentrepreneurs, especially those who are among the persistent poor, often require services beyond training and access to credit. These relationships also increase a program's visibility and reach, which may help it build legitimacy and political clout. Experience to date with these relationships suggests that microenterprise program officials, funders, and policymakers need to consider four basic points when making decisions concerning whether and how to structure and fund programs.

All partnerships involve trade-offs. Although the experiences of Women's Initiative and Working Capital provide a generally optimistic picture of interprogram networks, relationships always involve conflict, compromise, and negotiation. The relationships do not simply add capacity to microenterprise programs; they also entail a considerable amount of work. Collaboration, therefore, should not function as a code word for downsizing. Interprogram networking may place a strain on existing activity and drain resources from the core program. According to Bennett Harrison and Hector Cordero-Guzman, CBOs and funders tend to believe that "the formation and management of alliance relationships effectively *substitutes* for the internal capacity of CDCs and other community-based organizations," whereas in reality "internal capacity building and external network engagement should be understood as *complementary* processes."[18] Microenterprise programs should therefore enter into these relationships only after careful consideration. In fact, the programs may need to attain a level of maturity in their core activities before entering into relationships with other organizations and institutions, particularly when such interaction is not built into the structure of the program, as it is at Working Capital.

Intra- and interprogram networks are mutually reinforcing. Both Women's Initiative and Working Capital demonstrate that interaction between networks inside and outside the program forms a virtuous cycle. That is to say, the empowerment of borrowers that occurs through intraprogram networks creates access to other institutions, and that access is further reinforced through the formation of interprogram networks. The learning that occurs as a result of the interaction between these other institutions and microenterprise programs makes them more open to borrowers. Figure 6-1 illustrates this cycle.

18. Harrison and Cordero-Guzman (1996).

Figure 6-1. *Virtuous Cycles of Microenterprise Programs*

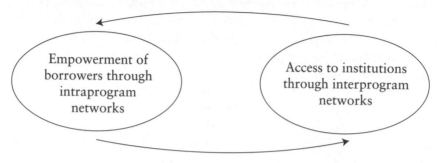

Networks are difficult to evaluate. Some of the difficulties related to evaluation were discussed in chapter 4. Program organizers must find ways to make the work that microenterprise programs do to build social capital more visible. The indicators that policymakers and funders tend to notice do not tell the whole story. Program evaluation must rely on alternative, "soft" indicators, such as increases in community activity, increased individual self-esteem, and greater family stability, as well as more traditional "hard" outcomes, such as jobs created and changes in income. Focusing on only one or the other misses the richness and complexity of what the programs accomplish. Furthermore, attention must be given to evaluation over the long term, through comprehensive, longitudinal studies. The benefits of program participation may not become fully evident for several years; they may even be intergenerational. By raising the self-esteem, positive outlook, and civic participation of the head of household, the programs must also be having some effect on the children in that household. Some of the participants in my research discussed making plans and setting goals with their children; many others were working with neighborhood youth. More research should be undertaken to demonstrate what kinds of relationships yield what kinds of payoffs.

Some current policies motivate the creation and maintenance of networks. Many banks fulfill Community Reinvestment Act requirements through collaboration with microenterprise programs. It is doubtful that they would be as interested in participating were it not for CRA. The Clinton administration's Empowerment Zone/Enterprise Community (EZEC) program has led many cities (Oakland is one) to create one-stop shops for entrepreneurs that reinforce relationships between microenterprise programs and related organizations. Many cities also allocate some of their CDBG funds to microenterprise programs, helping to forge links between programs and local government. In a time when economic development and social welfare programs are suffering severe cuts, it is important to highlight the ways in which these programs are contributing to community building in order to protect them from further reduction.

Conclusion

The networks of relationships that Women's Initiative and Working Capital have inspired build social capital through the trust that intraprogram relationships achieve and the alteration of norms that interprogram relationships foster. Unfortunately, the scale of this activity is far from what is necessary to transform communities. Building social capital is a very long process even in relatively advantaged communities. In inner cities that have suffered declining federal resources, structural economic change, and capital flight, and in which institutions are overburdened and lack resources, the task of building social capital is Herculean. Still, the kinds of changes that microenterprise programs bring about in the ways that individuals and institutions interact are important first steps. Building network-creating elements into other public and private programs located in disadvantaged communities would fortify this effort and increase the chances for real economic and political change.[19]

19. For example, the federal EZEC program has attempted to build in mechanisms for creating such networks. Cities that applied were required to submit plans that demonstrated coordination of government agencies, the private sector, and nonprofit organizations. This program is too young to have generated much research, but early evidence suggests that results of these efforts have been mixed.

SEVEN   *Conclusion:*
Potential and Pitfalls

P<small>AST ATTEMPTS TO ADDRESS</small> persistent poverty have had one great weakness: they have tended to shift attention away from its true causes. Some policymakers, assuming that persistent poverty is a monolithic problem, have sought big solutions, a silver bullet. They have missed the true complexity of the problem. Combating poverty is not just a matter of formulating specific poverty policies and programs. A host of other policies—education, health care, housing, child care, and others—need strengthening, too. Moreover, they all need greater coordination. Another failing of previous policy has been the tendency to separate structural economic issues from antipoverty issues. The goal of welfare reform is to move public assistance recipients into the work force, but that requires a great number of low-skill jobs that pay a family wage. Part-time, temporary, and seasonal employment that pays minimum wage and offers no benefits is much more the norm. Antipoverty policy has remained disconnected from economic trends.

Yet another failing is that the United States simply does not spend enough money to address the magnitude of this problem. Contributions to many programs are so small in relation to need that they are mostly symbolic. Finally, a large part of the urban poverty problem lies in deeply embedded discrimination based on gender, race, and other variables for which there is no easy or obvious policy solution. Policy can help to mask the symptoms of discrimination, but it cannot remove its roots.

Microenterprise programs are not the answer to the poverty problem. They do, however, expose people to the opportunities offered and con-

126

straints imposed by the new economy. They also avoid the traps just described. In addition, they exemplify the kind of structure and philosophy antipoverty programs would do well to emulate, for they recognize that routes into and out of poverty are multiple and complex. Microenterprise programs build on the reality of current economic conditions. They target disenfranchised groups and strengthen the attachment of their clients to the economy. Innovative approaches to ameliorating poverty are needed now more than ever. And because the federal safety net has been severely retracted, states are hungrier than ever for new ideas that work.

Moving beyond the Myths

A few words are in order about the misperceptions in which current policy is mired, especially as they relate to the microenterprise strategy. These myths prevent programs from realizing their full potential. Program organizers and field experts must work to debunk them so that the strategy can be supported appropriately.

MYTH 1. *Microentrepreneurs need credit more than anything else.* Credit is a necessary ingredient of microenterprise development, but it is far from the only one. The success of these programs derives from their provision of a wide range of resources—through networks, training, and support—that include but are not limited to credit. This emphasis on credit, to the neglect of operating support, arises in part because U.S. microenterprise programs are regularly compared with the models in the developing world that motivated the U.S. movement. The fact is, the microenterprise strategy is more expensive to implement in the United States than it is abroad. And although credit is an important aspect of what these programs do, it is the primary focus of only a few programs. The supplementary supports provided by microenterprise programs drive the strategy.

MYTH 2. *Success equals starting a business.* Many people who attend microenterprise programs do not start businesses. They may have been attracted to self-employment but perhaps learned that their business idea was not strong enough to provide them with the income they required. Or they may have come to the microenterprise program as a last resort after having been frustrated by other programs. For many clients, participation in a microenterprise program sets off a process that opens up many new opportunities, only one of which is business creation. Although evidence on what happens once people leave microenterprise programs is mostly anecdotal, program organizers count helping people make the right decision not to start a business as a successful outcome. Most clients leave programs feeling more secure and in control of their economic futures, regardless of whether they start businesses.

MYTH 3. *Business creation is a one-time event.* Starting and stabilizing a small business is a long-term effort. It is not an event that takes place all at once. Some participants drop out of programs and return once they have their lives in order. Others pursue extra training before starting. Some generate self-employment income from several sources without focusing on, or before focusing on, a single business. Most struggle for a long time before making a profit. Moving from idea to viable business can take years. This process is valuable in and of itself, and the spillover effects it produces change the people and places microenterprise programs serve in important ways.

MYTH 4. *Microbusinesses grow into big businesses.* Every microenterprise program has a few success stories of people who started sole proprietorships, received a $5,000 loan, and now employ a large work force and make hefty profits. These businesses are the exception. Most microbusinesses stay small, mainly because their owners want to stay small. They started the business so that they could spend more time with their children, and they keep it small for the same reason. Or they use the business as a way to generate supplemental income for the household. They may not want to take on the added responsibility of managing employees or operating a storefront business. Microenterprise programs do not generate large numbers of jobs, nor do they add greatly to the tax base of an area. They do provide critical income to households, often boosting them above the poverty line.

Supporting Microenterprise Programs

Before the microenterprise strategy can approach its potential, it will need many forms of support from policymakers at all levels of government and from funders. That support must be grounded in the recognition that the myths just presented are false.

Support Operating Expenses

Program directors and field experts across the board have stated that microenterprise programs need more money to support their general operation. The program directors I interviewed agreed that the programs are often as much about training as they are about credit; policymakers and funders are taking longer to recognize this fact. Most microenterprise programs have had little trouble raising funds to make loans. They face much more difficulty generating dollars to support the training activities and general operations. At Women's Initiative the classes are continually oversubscribed, while the loan fund is underused. Many field experts believe that the federal government could provide critical help. According to Welthy Soni, director of a program called Business Start based in Appalachia,

> The ideal place for the federal government to help is in the whole area of capacity building, helping programs to be sustainable. Getting loan money does not seem to be a significant problem. Banks are willing to lend money. Sustainability money, capacity money, is critical and it's a relatively small investment.

Some funders and policymakers are more interested in contributing to loan funds than in supporting the training, one-on-one counseling, technical assistance, and mentoring activities that are critical to helping people become successful entrepreneurs. Policymakers who want to support the microenterprise strategy for welfare recipients must invest in the training. The programs that serve people on a very low income require even greater funding for training and support than do programs whose populations run into fewer barriers to success. Programs that serve the poorest people, such as ISED, Women's Initiative, and WHEDCO, report that the welfare population often requires more training and a higher number of hours of follow-up support.

Educate Economic Development Planners and Policymakers

Policy and program officials fall into three categories in relation to their views on microenterprise: some are working with the microenterprise strategy and understand both its potential and its limitations; some know little or nothing about the microenterprise strategy; and some claim to have tried to use it but believe that it was a failure. Those in the latter two categories do not know enough about the microenterprise strategy, and many of them confuse U.S. programs with their cousins in the developing world. The microenterprise strategy is young in comparison with most traditional poverty alleviation and economic development strategies, and understanding among policymakers is uneven at best.

All of the program directors interviewed who have achieved strong relationships with government officials have done so by educating them. Luck has played a large role thus far. Women's Initiative formed a critical relationship with the San Francisco Mayor's Office on Community Development from the beginning. ISED has strong partnerships with its state departments of economic development and human services. The public officials interviewed who put little stock in the microenterprise strategy tended to espouse the same myths that people in the field are working to debunk. Policymakers need to be educated about what, specifically, microenterprise programs can do and must employ them appropriately in their larger visions for poverty alleviation and economic development.

Integrate Microenterprise Programs into a Larger Policy Solution

To reiterate, microenterprise programs will not solve the poverty problem. They are, however, one key piece of a larger puzzle. To be effective, they must be packaged with other complementary programs specific to the place, its people, and their needs. Coordination among the programs is extremely important. Jack Litzenberg, of the Charles Stewart Mott Foundation—an important funder of microenterprise programs—believes that the ideal program is

> one that has adapted to its own culture, and that connects with people who lend at higher amounts. It is one that understands that there needs to be a continuum of capital in low-income communities. It is sustainable even if it is not self-sufficient. It should also have a feature of providing a support system to the client, and it should collaborate well with the community. Successful programs do not try to do everything themselves.

Some programs, such as ISED, work closely with their state departments of social welfare and economic development. Others participate in regional economic development organizations that help coordinate these sorts of efforts. The quality of relationships between state and local officials and microenterprise programs varies and depends greatly on how receptive local officials are to integrating the microenterprise strategy into their larger mission.

Applying the Lessons

The recent changes in the economic development and social welfare fields described in chapter 4 motivate the creation of microenterprise programs, and the lessons learned from them offer some hope as they light the way to a new direction in policy. Because the programs developed out of grass roots efforts, they possess unique characteristics that may help inform state policy as Temporary Assistance for Needy Families replaces Aid to Families with Dependent Children, and as each state begins to think creatively about how to combat its particular poverty problem.

First, the locally initiated nature of programs such as microenterprise development has made them well suited to the context in which they operate and sensitive to the needs of their particular constituency. This local orientation has allowed them to stay very flexible, boosting training capacity, broadening or narrowing the target population, increasing loan size ceilings, and so forth, as appropriate. If public sector funding for microenterprise and other new strategies continues to increase, as it seems likely to do, fund use should also be supervised at the most local level possible. Local government institutions and local representatives of federal institutions are in a better position to work with microenterprise programs than Washington-based officials. Successful programs are responsive to the contexts in which they operate, including the economic landscape and the characteristics of the labor force. State intermediaries, a new form of organization in the microenterprise field, are another promising venue through which to route support. These intermediaries raise federal funds to support microenterprise programs, use those funds to leverage state funds, and channel them to local microenterprise programs. Intermediary organizations are generally staffed by people who worked for a microenterprise program before. They relieve some of the pressure to raise funds from the local programs and relieve funders of the burden of evaluation.

Second, antipoverty policy must begin from an understanding of the diversity of the group at which it is directed. Microenterprise programs are well suited to helping the more motivated of the persistently poor. The stories of the people who pursue microentrepreneurship underscore the need to recognize that the poor are extremely heterogeneous and will require many kinds of ladders to climb out of poverty. Too often, policy efforts become stuck on stereotypes that fit only a small percentage of poor people instead of focusing on others such as the working poor who are also more ready to benefit from assistance. The fact that microenterprise programs are only helping a very small group also places them in danger of being cut out of policy and funding, whereas they should be recognized for their effectiveness on one part of the larger population.

Third, evaluation must evolve along with the strategies themselves. To reconstruct antipoverty policy and make it more effective, legislators will have to change not just the policies themselves, but also the way in which they are evaluated. The indicators that policymakers employ in the case of microenterprise programs fall far short of telling the whole story of what these programs accomplish. Comprehensive, longitudinal evaluations are often said to be too costly. Thus far, evaluation efforts have failed to keep pace with advances in practice. To evaluate these programs appropriately, it will be necessary to look at social welfare indicators such as increases in individual self-esteem and family stability, as well as traditional economic development outcomes such as jobs created and changes in income. Focusing on only one or the other kind of indicator misses the richness and complexity of what these programs accomplish. It will also be necessary to look at the outcomes these programs produce over the years. The problem of persistent poverty in this country appears to be intergenerational. Therefore it seems reasonable to assume that potential solutions must be evaluated over the very long term.

Fourth, the experience of microenterprise programs illustrates how the lack of policy coordination can diminish potential effectiveness. Although government financial support will certainly strengthen the viability of these programs, other policies work against microenterprise development, making it difficult for low-income people to think of self-employment as a workable solution. Chapter 5 points out the income-packaging strategies of low-income entrepreneurs as well as their difficulties in obtaining benefits such as health insurance and child care. The workfare programs of many states do not accept participation in microenterprise programs as worthy use of recipients' time. In addition, many programs see themselves as the first lender, expecting the microentrepreneur to begin working with mainstream financial institutions after borrowing successfully from the program. Despite the 1977 Community Reinvestment Act, which requires banks to serve fully the communities in which they operate, discrimination based on gender, race, and class continues to exclude people. Thus the policy infrastructure needed to make microenterprise programs stepping-stones rather than permanent havens does not exist. Furthermore, access to training and credit cannot exist in a vacuum. The need for additional universal social policies providing health care and child care is amplified in the case of microentrepreneurs.

Fifth, antipoverty policy and programs must provide a more positive incentive than the threat of the loss of benefits before people will move to change their situation. Those who have lived in distressed communities for a long time have witnessed the rise and fall, the coming and going, of countless programs and people supposedly working to help them. Many remain skeptical and unwilling to give so much of their energy to an activity that might not make things better. In this case, perception may equal reality. Job-training policy relies on the assumption that employment opportunities are plentiful, if only everyone had proper training. Even when these programs do match people with jobs, beneficiaries of training often have little say in what kind of training they will receive and in what jobs they will be placed after going through programs. Many are placed in jobs that pay so little that, after accounting for the additional child care and transportation expenses that must be incurred, recipients are economically better off collecting welfare. The time limits that welfare reform imposes make that option less possible. Although many states have initiated creative programs to help move welfare recipients to work, jobs with room for advancement that pay a living wage are still hard to find.

Although microenterprise programs are not suitable for everyone, they do help create the conditions for change for an important part of the poor population. People are responsive to the idea of running their own businesses. Self-employment allows them to choose their own jobs, by drawing on and building their own skills and interests rather than trying to fit into a preexisting program that offers little security for the future.

In addition, coupling training with the possibility of gaining access to credit not only helps people start businesses that have growth potential, but also enables them to make other strides forward, such as improving a bad credit rating and learning to take control of their finances. Micro-enterprise programs have been marketed as programs that enable disenfranchised people to enter the mainstream economy by creating their own jobs. Borrowers participate in other ways as well, for example, as consumers. Also, the kind of training participants receive is applicable to a wide range of life and work situations because it is geared toward running a business, which requires skills in finance, management, and sales, as well as economic literacy. Other programs must similarly engage those they target.

Perhaps one of the most important things that microenterprise programs accomplish is that they help change people's attitudes by creating forward motion, giving them the hope they need to believe that they can take charge of their own lives. By helping people begin to think strategically about creating better futures for themselves and providing them with the tools necessary to make that happen, these programs shift the focus of attention from maintenance to investment. Placing this orientation at the center of future antipoverty policy is certainly something worth striving toward. To do so, policymakers will have to define poverty more broadly than as a function of income. And they will have to understand poverty as a function of assets and access to resources.

Imbuing antipoverty policies with an asset-creating orientation and steering public programs toward investment rather than maintenance may also allow policymakers and their constituents to take a longer view of the poverty issue. Persistent poverty is a bigger problem than income provision alone can handle. The provision of income in the United States is insufficient. It is a short-term solution that helps people cope with everyday needs, but it does not help them escape poverty. The transition from poverty to self-sufficiency can only take place if people have the tools and skills they need to develop. Access to resources such as credit and training creates opportunities with far greater potential than the benefits typical transfer programs provide. The important point for policymakers to remember is that it will take time to reap the rewards of this new form of investment.

APPENDIX *Methodology*

THIS APPENDIX LAYS out the research design of this project. It includes explanations of why the methods used were chosen, what the data consist of, and how data collection was carried out. In addition, it discusses the steps taken to ensure the reliability of the results given the methods chosen. The appendix first outlines the research agenda and its broad goals. Next, it explains the choice of the case study method and lays out the logic for selecting the programs and cities studied. The discussion then moves to the data and the ways in which they were collected. The interviews are discussed at length because they lie at the heart of the research. In conclusion, I raise the issues of representativeness, biases, and subjectivities.

Research Agenda

This research was intended to provide a fine-grained description of a new strategy—microenterprise development—that does not fit neatly into either the social welfare or the economic development category because it includes aspects of both. Such a description serves several purposes. First, it helps place microenterprise programs in the historical context of economic development and social welfare strategies, showing the different traditions out of which the microenterprise hybrid has grown. Second, by making the recipients of the programs the focus of the research, it provides a unique lens onto poor peoples' lives, showing how they obtain access to such resources as credit, which are largely unavailable to the poor. This kind of description, which begins with the individual, also tells what these programs do for people as individuals, rather than as aggregates, in the way that the majority of evaluations do.

The research was designed to tell two kinds of stories. The first deals with the program. It is the story of this hybridized type of program that resides somewhere between the traditional fields of economic development and social welfare. Telling it involved learning enough about the historical directions of these two fields to set microenterprise programs accurately within this context. It also entailed documenting the social, political, and economic conditions that allowed for the creation and emergence of strategies with this kind of orientation.

The second kind of story deals with the individual. It documents the histories of poor people who are trying very hard to escape poverty and are using these particular programs as vehicles to help them help themselves. Telling their stories broadens our understanding of poverty. Obtaining better information on this segment of the urban poor population enriches our understanding of the circumstances that lead to poverty and the range of strategies that poor people piece together to survive.

Choice of Case Study Method

Several factors made the case study method the most appropriate one for conducting this research in a way that fulfilled the agenda and the goals described in the introductory chapter. First, case studies allow the kind of in-depth analysis that the goals of this project call for. This research is exploratory and therefore the questions that need to be asked are about processes and relationships. The qualitative methods employed are sensitive to subtlety, conflict, and multiple viewpoints. Second, the explanatory nature of the research questions posed, which ask *how* microenterprise programs work and *why* they have emerged as the latest answer to the urban poverty problem, is best suited to the use of case studies.[1] Third, the case study method allows one to incorporate a wide range of data. One goal is to collect a great deal of information from a variety of sources to

1. According to Robert Yin, "case studies are the preferred strategy when 'how' or 'why' questions are being posed, when the investigator has little control over events, and when the focus is on a contemporary phenomenon within some real-life context" (1989, p. 13). This study of microenterprise programs closely matches Yin's description.

describe very specifically the way various microenterprise programs work and how they are perceived by individuals and institutions. The specific kinds of data used in this study are discussed later.

Detailed descriptions of the microenterprise programs also lay a solid foundation for future research such as large-scale surveys, longitudinal studies, and comparisons with programs in other countries. Multiple case studies were done to gain a sense of the spectrum of ways in which the microenterprise strategy has been employed and the range of approaches that fall under this umbrella. By looking at five cases, it was possible to examine the differences in program philosophies and how these relate to program contexts, as well as the similarities that bring them under one label. Similarities that held across all five programs provided a base from which to generalize to a larger group of programs and make policy recommendations.

Choice of Programs and Cities

The decision was made to look only at microenterprise programs in areas with a substantial poor population and those that have been in operation for a minimum of three years. This eliminated many possible choices. It seemed logical to consider programs located in the older industrial metropolises of the Northeast and Midwest, where urban poverty is firmly entrenched. Three of the five programs—Accion New York, WHEDCO, and Working Capital in Boston—operate in northeastern cities. Women's Initiative and ISED were selected as the fourth and fifth cases for several reasons. First, Women's Initiative operates in a West Coast city (San Francisco–Oakland) and ISED operates statewide in Iowa, providing a contrast to the other three. Although the problem of persistent poverty may be regional in its most chronic manifestation, it is by no means confined to northeastern cities. Second, both Women's Initiative and ISED have been leaders in policy change, and getting a sense of how microenterprise organizers perceive their situation within the policy environment was an important part of this research.

Each program relates specifically to the goals of the research project in that each approaches the problem of poor people's access to resources in a different way. The decision to look at programs that differ significantly accords with the desire to document the variety of ways in which this strategy has emerged and been implemented across the country.

Methods of Data Collection

A broad range of primary and secondary data were collected to fulfill the research agenda and maximize the usefulness of the case study method. The data fall into four categories: in-depth interviews, existing program data, nonparticipant observation, and a closer look at the interviews.

In-Depth Interviews

In-depth interviews were conducted with each of three groups: board and staff members from each program, clients-borrowers at each program, and officials at connected institutions.[2] Board and staff interviews concentrated on board and staff interpretations of their programs' mission and goals and their assessment of what their programs have and have not accomplished. Interviews with clients-borrowers at each program were much broader in scope, and covered questions ranging from the borrower's entrepreneurial history to his or her relationship with program staff. Interviews with officials at connected institutions were designed to obtain the perspectives of microenterprise experts; program funders, public and private; and small business lenders and borrowers in traditional financial institutions. In addition, interviews were conducted with executive directors of other microenterprise programs, field experts, funders, and policymakers.

Existing Program Data

This category consists of program data such as budgets, organizational charts, historical statistics on client base and loan fund activity, and internal reports and evaluations; externally generated research, including studies conducted by other researchers and grantmaking institutions; and state and local interpretations of relevant policy such as the Community Reinvestment Act and AFDC/TANF regulations. Although I specifically chose programs that had kept records of clients since the inception of the program, the quality and accessibility of information varied significantly from one program to another. When I began my fieldwork, both Women's Initiative and Working Capital had recently completed surveys and analyses

2. Accion does not have a board at the local level, although discussions are under way about whether to form one.

of past borrowers. Accion was in the process of transferring client records from paper to computer when I arrived.[3]

Nonparticipant Observation

I spent a great deal of time at each program site and at client businesses. I attended classes, consulting sessions, borrower group meetings, and loan committee meetings to get a sense of the day-to-day operation of each program and obtain a more complete picture of lender-borrower relations. In most instances I conducted interviews at borrowers' homes or businesses, which allowed me to get a better feel for the businesses financed through the loans.

A Closer Look at the Interview Piece

Because in-depth interviews constitute the core of the research conducted for this project, it makes sense to discuss in more specific terms how the fieldwork was approached and how I dealt with problems as they arose. The choice of in-depth interviewing as the primary research method arose out of my recognition that, historically, much social science research includes the goal of quantification, which in turn requires fitting people into categories. Although this kind of research is necessary for generating and assessing policy, it carries with it the problem of equating individuals with the categories into which they fit, which often perpetuates harmful stereotypes. The finer-grained methods that this research used helped to humanize quantitative analysis. Because they are expensive, time-consuming, and accorded lesser status in academic and policymaking circles, these methods often go unused.[4]

Interviews with borrowers posed the greatest potential problems because some of the questions dealt with sensitive information, and it was therefore essential for me to gain borrowers' trust relatively quickly. Each organization introduced me to borrowers and reassured them, when necessary, that I would not use the information I obtained against them. Some of the interview subjects were undocumented immigrants, and others were

3. I agreed to help Accion New York create a database in return for gaining access to the program for my research.

4. For additional insight into how traditional social science methods have proven detrimental to our conception of the urban poor, see Katz (1989, esp. pp. 169 and following).

"bending" AFDC/TANF regulations, making it risky for them to talk to me. One woman who is operating her business under the table while she collects welfare to repair her credit record, agreed to meet with me only after she checked with her business consultant to ascertain that I was not a spy. On the whole, I believe that I succeeded in gaining borrowers' trust. Most participants seemed to enjoy telling me their stories, and many told me that it was a useful process for them.

With some wording changes, many of the questions asked in the interview format could have been asked in a survey. Survey instruments, while they have the undeniable advantage of producing data that are amenable to statistical treatment, are rigid and therefore more suited to answering narrow questions than to providing descriptive information and answering broader questions. The microenterprise field is new and unstudied enough to require a more flexible approach. In in-depth interviews the interviewer becomes the instrument. She enters into the interview with specific categories and questions, but she can also allow the interviewee to redefine the questions, shift the categories of analysis, and bring in new categories of analysis. The style of interviewing I employed conforms most closely to Herbert Rubin and Irene Rubin's concept of interviews as guided conversations.[5] Traditional evaluation research tends to make assumptions about how program staff and borrowers define success for programs, borrowers, and their businesses without talking to borrowers themselves. These assumptions have helped feed the debates that this research attempts to inform, or at least to enrich.

To meet some of the goals of this research, I found it necessary to break some of the rules of textbook interviewing. One of the rules is that the interviewee is an object of study that gives information and that the interviewer should extract information while giving out as little as possible. The one-sided interaction that results from this model creates a kind of hierarchy in which my own ethics would not allow me to participate. The textbook argument is that if different interviewees have different information about the interviewer, a bias will be introduced into the research. I controlled for this bias as much as possible by giving out answers to commonly asked questions (which I learned from doing pilot interviews) at the outset. These included why I was doing the research and what the interviews would be used for. Interviewees also often wanted to know more about me: where I was studying, whether I had ever run a business,

5. Rubin and Rubin (1997).

why I was interested in this topic. When these and other questions came up during the interviews, I answered as honestly as I could.

To give interviewees a greater sense of control, I took time at the beginning of the interview to explain how I would use tapes and notes. I also sent copies of my transcripts to each participant for review. I allowed them to clarify anything or to withhold any part of the information from publication. In addition, I gave participants my telephone number and told them to call if they had other thoughts or questions after the interview. At the end of each interview, I asked participants if there was anything they thought I should have asked that I had not, if there was anything they wanted to add or felt I should know, and if they had any questions for me. Relinquishing some of the control within the interview allowed me not only to level the hierarchy somewhat but also to produce better research. Creating an interaction based on give and take made the interviewees more comfortable with interjecting, offering supplementary information, and redefining issues and questions. In addition, as Ann Oakley states, "Personal involvement is more than dangerous bias—it is the condition under which people come to know each other and to admit others into their lives."[6] Some participants wrote me months after their interview to let me know how they were doing.

To minimize the cultural distance between interviewer and interviewee, I hired a Colombian graduate student to conduct the interviews with Accion clients. As a native Spanish speaker, Sandra's ability to communicate with these borrowers was better than mine. In addition, because I was not doing participant observation and did not have much time to establish trust, I came to the conclusion after speaking with Accion staff that borrowers were more likely to be open with Sandra than with me. In addition, as Oakley states, "Where both interviewer and interviewee share membership of the same minority group, the basis for equality may impress itself even more urgently on the interviewer's consciousness."[7] I believe, for example, that I obtained richer responses to my questions about the role of gender when I interviewed women than I would have as a man. Similarly, I believe that Sandra obtained better information from Latino interviewees about the role of ethnicity than I would have.

Although I did everything I could to address and lessen the power gap that exists between interviewer and interviewee, I could not eliminate it. It

6. Oakley (1981, p. 58).
7. Oakley (1981, p. 55).

is important to recognize, as Michael Burawoy states, that "being sensitive to power inequality doesn't remove it."[8] In the end it is my interpretation of the stories, numbers, and events I collected that is represented here.

I conducted initial fieldwork at Women's Initiative, Accion, and Working Capital between January and July 1994. During this period I conducted thirty-six interviews with program clients and twelve with program staff. I conducted the research for chapter 6 during the summer of 1996, returning to Women's Initiative and Working Capital to conduct an additional twenty interviews with clients and ten with program staff and key officials at affiliated programs and institutions. The fieldwork for chapter 5 was performed at Women's Initiative, ISED, and WHEDCO between August 1997 and January 1998. Thirty-five interviews with current or former welfare recipient–clients were conducted, as well as thirteen with program staff. Over the course of the entire research period, twenty-seven additional interviews were conducted with directors of other microenterprise programs, field experts, funders, and policymakers.

Representativeness

I attempted to make the cases chosen as representative as possible of the microenterprise strategy.

Representativeness among Programs

Although every program differs from every other in many ways, there are categories of characteristics that provide insight into the philosophy guiding a program, the kind of borrowers it attracts, and its future orientation. These characteristics include whether and how a program targets its services, how it is funded, how it weights training and lending functions, and whether it serves only existing businesses or includes start-ups. At the same time, it is not clear that, for example, studying one program that does group lending makes it possible to generalize to all programs that do group lending. It is always important to look closely at the marriage between a particular characteristic, such as targeting, and the philosophy of the program.

8. Burawoy (1991, p. 5).

Representativeness within Programs

My goal was to talk to as wide a range of entrepreneurs as possible. I therefore asked staff at all five programs for lists of borrowers that varied according to the following characteristics:[9] (1) gender, (2) race, (3) ethnicity, (4) type of business, (5) number of loans obtained, (6) size of loans, (7) home-based business versus off-site business, (8) socioeconomic status, and (9) satisfaction with program. I sought variety rather than randomness, both to obtain a sense of the range of life situations borrowers came from and to identify areas for further research.

To win the trust of borrowers and gain access to them, especially those who took substantial risks by participating in this research, it was necessary for me to work through the programs. I used program names when I called clients to schedule interviews, and broke the ice with Accion clients through a letter of introduction sent to clients by the director of the program. The problem with this approach was that it made me less likely to get access to those clients who had had trouble with their business or their loans. To counter this dynamic, I made it clear to potential participants that I did not work for the programs and that I would maintain the confidentiality of all information with which I was entrusted. Some borrowers, albeit few, were angry with programs and did not want anything further to do with them. They perceived talking to me as doing a favor for the program. Others facing similar situations used the interview as an opportunity to vent their anger and frustration, either seeing me as separate from the program, and therefore "safe," or hoping that their message would get back to those with whom they were upset. Given the existence of this kind of dynamic, this research is probably slightly biased toward those borrowers who were relatively satisfied with their microenterprise experience.

Biases and Subjectivities

All research is political. All research is based on the biases and assumptions of the researcher. Biases are not sins to be atoned for but rather pieces of baggage, inherited or acquired. Unlike baggage, however, biases cannot be left at the gate. And because they must necessarily be brought

---

9. Depending on the program, obviously, it was sometimes impossible to vary the subjects along one trait or another. For example, Women's Initiative serves only women.

on board, they must be acknowledged at the outset. As Michael Burawoy has stated, "The purpose of field work is not to strip ourselves of biases, for that is an illusory goal, nor to celebrate those biases as the authorial voice of the ethnographer, but rather to discover and perhaps change our biases through interaction with others."[10] This appendix seems to be an appropriate place to address that aspect of this research.

I began this project believing that, historically, most economic development policy directed at the urban poor had been misguided, that new strategies would have to look at the role of gender, class, and race, and that access to credit and training could play a crucial role in improving urban economic development policy. I chose to do work on this topic both because I am intellectually curious about the inner workings of the microenterprise strategy and its position within the larger context and history of urban economic development and poverty alleviation strategies, and because I believe that this kind of work can make an important contribution to policy. I therefore sought to establish a research situation that would allow me to participate in a dialogue with a particular segment of poor people who are using self-employment as a survival strategy.

Although I continue to believe that I went about doing my research with an open mind, I was surprised to realize that I had some preconceptions about the kinds of people and neighborhoods that lie at the heart of this research. I learned about these primarily during my interviews with program participants, and I thank them for challenging me. I remember learning about the Working Capital Borrower's Council in Metro Boston and all of the program work that this group was doing. Initially, I wondered why the program was not providing some of these services. Herb, who chairs the Borrower's Council, set me straight. "You have to sustain yourself," he told me. "You can't subsist on just grants and handouts, you know. You have to do something to sustain yourself . . . . Some of these other things maybe we should have to do, and I don't mind doing that because it's going to benefit me." Whereas I thought borrowers would want the program to take on this work, Herb explained to me how the program had given them opportunity, and that this was enough. In another instance, Nina, a Working Capital borrower, was talking to me about her desire to open a bakery where she could sell her cakes. Deciding where to locate would be a tough decision. "I live in a community that does not have the means to support my business. They can't support my family,"

10. Burawoy (1991, p. 4).

she said. She also worried about her children. I assumed that she meant that it would be good for the children to move to a safer neighborhood, but that was not at all what Nina meant. "I wouldn't want to move them out of here because this is where their culture is," she said. If she and her family were to leave, she was afraid that the children would miss out on an important community socialization process.

These anecdotes begin to describe the ways in which conducting this research brought me face to face with my own biases. More important, perhaps, these stories also begin to reveal the complex circumstances surrounding the lives of poor, urban entrepreneurs.

References

Acosta, Sandra. 1995. "Accion New York: An Outreach Plan." Unpublished report prepared for the New School for Social Research Graduate School of Management and Urban Policy and Accion New York.

Bates, Timothy. 1995. "Why Do Minority Business Development Programs Generate So Little Minority Business Development?" *Economic Development Quarterly* 9 (1): 3–14.

Bornstein, David. 1996. *The Price of a Dream.* Simon and Schuster.

Briggs, Xavier de Souza. 1998. "Brown Kids in White Suburbs: Housing Mobility and the Many Faces of Social Capital." *Housing Policy Debate* 9 (1): 177–221.

Burawoy, Michael. 1991. *Ethnography Unbound: Power and Resistance in the Modern Metropolis.* University of California Press.

Buruss, William, and Katherine Stearns. 1997. *Building a Model: ACCION's Approach to Microenterprise in the United States.* Washington, D.C.: ACCION International.

Charles Stewart Mott Foundation. 1990. *Small Steps towards Big Dreams.* Flint, Mich.

———. 1993. *Small Steps towards Big Dreams: 1993 Update.* Flint, Mich.

———. 1994. *Small Steps towards Big Dreams: 1994 Update.* Flint, Mich.

Clark, Peggy, and Tracy Huston. 1993. *Assisting the Smallest Businesses: Assessing Microenterprise Development as a Strategy for Boosting Poor Communities.* An interim report of the Self-Employment Learning Project. Washington, D.C.: Aspen Institute.

Clark, Peggy, and Amy J. Kays. 1995. *Enabling Entrepreneurship: Microenterprise Development in the United States, Baseline Year Report of the Self-Employment Learning Project.* Washington, D.C.: Aspen Institute.

Clinton, William Jefferson. 1997. *The State of Small Business. A Report of the President.* Washington, D.C.: U.S. Government Printing Office.

Cooper, Candy. 1992. "A Piece of the Dream." *Image,* the Magazine of the *San Francisco Examiner,* August 23.

147

Corporation for Enterprise Development. 1993. *AFDC and Microenterprise: Working with Your State to Address Regulatory Barriers.* Washington, D.C.

Department of Housing and Urban Development. "Designation of Empowerment Zones and Enterprise Communities: Interim Rules and Notices," FR Doc. 94-1148. *Federal Register* 59 (January 18, 1994): 2686–2712.

Edgcomb, Elaine, Joyce Klein, and Peggy Clark. 1996. *The Practice of Microenterprise in the U.S.: Strategies, Costs, and Effectiveness.* Self-Employment Learning Project. Washington, D.C.: Aspen Institute.

Edin, Kathryn, and Laura Lein. 1997. *Making Ends Meet: How Single Mothers Survive Welfare and Low-Wage Work.* Russell Sage Foundation.

Garfinkel, Irwin, and Sara McLanahan. 1994. "Single-Mother Families, Economic Insecurity, and Government Policy." In *Confronting Poverty: Prescriptions for Change,* edited by Sheldon H. Danziger, Gary D. Sandefur, and Daniel H. Weinberg, 205–25. Russell Sage Foundation.

Harrison, Bennett, and Hector Cordero-Guzman. 1996. "Untangling the Ties That Bind: Organizational Capacity and Performance in CBO Workforce Development Networks." Work plan submitted to the Urban Poverty Program of the Ford Foundation.

Hartmann, Heidi. 1987. "Changes in Women's Economic and Family Roles in Post–World War II United States." In *Women, Households, and the Economy,* edited by Lourdes Beneria and Catherine R. Stimpson, 33–64. Rutgers University Press.

Himes, Cristina, and Lisa J. Servon. 1998. *Measuring Client Success: An Evaluation of ACCION's Impact on Microenterprises in the United States.* U.S. Issues Series, no. 2. Washington, D.C.: ACCION International.

Katz, Michael B. 1989. *The Undeserving Poor: From the War on Poverty to the War on Welfare.* Pantheon Books.

Klein, Joyce. 1994. "The Status of the Microenterprise Field." Unpublished report to the Corporation for Enterprise Development.

McKee, Katherine. 1990. "The Great Balancing Act: Sustaining an Alternative Financial Institution." *Entrepreneurial Economy Review* 8 (May–June): 14–17.

McLenighan, Valjean, and Jean Pogge. 1991. *The Business of Self-Sufficiency: Microcredit Programs in the United States.* Chicago: Woodstock Institute.

Mt. Auburn Associates. 1994. "An Evaluation of the Working Capital Microenterprise Lending Program." Submitted to the Institute for Cooperative Community Development, New Hampshire College.

Novogratz, Jacqueline. 1992. *Hopeful Change: The Potential of Microenterprise Programs as a Community Revitalization Intervention.* New York: Rockefeller Foundation.

Oakley, Ann. 1981. "Interviewing Women: A Contradiction in Terms." In *Doing Feminist Research,* edited by Helen Roberts, 30–61. Boston: Routledge & Kegan Paul.

Pearce, Diana M. 1989. "The Feminization of Poverty: A Second Look." Paper prepared for the American Sociological Meetings, San Francisco.

———. 1990. "Welfare Is Not for Women: Why the War on Poverty Cannot

Conquer the Feminization of Poverty." In *Women, the State, and Welfare*, edited by Linda Gordon, 265–79. University of Wisconsin Press.

Putnam, Robert D. 1993. *Making Democracy Work: Civic Traditions in Modern Italy.* Princeton University Press.

Raheim, Salome, and Alter, Catherine Foster. 1995. *Self-Employment Investment Demonstration Final Evaluation Report Part I: Participant Survey.* University of Iowa School of Social Work.

Rubin, Herbert J., and Irene S. Rubin. 1997. *Qualitative Interviewing: The Art of Hearing Data.* Newbury Park, Calif.: Sage Publications.

Self-Employment Learning Project. 1991. "Interim Lessons from the Self-Employment Investment Demonstration." Washington, D.C.: Corporation for Enterprise Development.

———. 1993. "Microenterprise Briefing Packet: Facts and Figures on Seven U.S. Microenterprise Development Programs." Washington, D.C.: Aspen Institute.

———. 1995. "Microenterprise Assistance: What Are We Learning about Results?" Washington, D.C.: Aspen Institute Economic Opportunities Program.

Servon, Lisa J. 1992. "Microcredit in the U.S.: An Alternative Economic Survival Strategy." *Berkeley Planning Journal* 7: 148–56.

———. 1994. "The Institutionalization of Microcredit: Moving Forward by Looking Back." *Economic Development Commentary* 18 (Fall 1994): 23–29.

———. 1996. "Microenterprise Programs and Women: Credit as Individual Empowerment." *Journal of Developmental Entrepreneurship* 1 (Summer): 31–54.

———. 1997. "Microenterprise Programs in U.S. Inner Cities: Economic Development or Social Welfare?" *Economic Development Quarterly* 11 (May): 166–80.

———. 1998a. "Helping Poor Women Achieve Self-Sufficiency through Self-Employment: The Potential of U.S. Microenterprise Programs." Working Paper 98-06. Washington, D.C.: Research Institute for Small and Emerging Business.

———. 1998b. "Why Pursue Self-Employment?: The Range of Options for Disadvantaged Entrepreneurs." Paper prepared for the Association of Collegiate Schools of Planning Conference, Pasadena.

Servon, Lisa J., and Timothy Bates. 1998. "Microenterprise as an Exit Route from Poverty: Recommendations for Programs and Policy Makers." *Journal of Urban Affairs* 20 (4): 419–41.

Severens, C. Alexander, and Amy Kays. 1997. *1996 Directory of U.S. Microenterprise Programs.* Self-Employment Learning Project. Washington, D.C.: Apsen Institute.

Spalter-Roth, Roberta M., Heidi I. Hartmann, and Beverly Burr. 1994. "Income Insecurity: The Failure of Unemployment Insurance to Reach Working AFDC Mothers." Paper presented at the Conference on Employment Law and Unemployment Compensation, Washington, D.C., March 20.

Spalter-Roth, Roberta, Enrique Soto, and Lily Zandniapour. 1994. *Microenterprise and Women: The Viability of Self-Employment as a Strategy for Alleviating Poverty.* Washington, D.C.: Institute for Women's Policy Research.

Stack, Carol B. 1974. *All Our Kin: Strategies for Survival in a Black Community.* Harper and Row.

Tinker, Irene. 1989. "Credit for Poor Women: Necessary, But Not Always Sufficient for Change." *Marga* 10 (2): 31–48.

———. n.d. "The Human Economy of Microentrepreneurs." Unpublished paper.

Yin, Robert K. 1989. *Case Study Research: Design and Methods.* Newbury Park, Calif.: Sage Publications.

Index